WHEN THE SMOKE CLEARS

WHEN THE SMOKE CLEARS

Your User's Guide To Prepare You
For The Insurance Game!

Anthony Astone
&
Steve Boydstun

IME Publishing Group
www.IMEPublishingGroup.com

Warning—Disclaimer

*Disclaimer and Terms of Use: The Authors and Publisher has strived to be as accurate and
complete as possible in the creation of this book, notwithstanding the fact that they do not
warrant or represent at any time that the contents within are accurate due to the rapidly changing
nature of the Internet. While all attempts have been made to verify information provided in this
publication, the Authors and Publisher assumes no responsibility for errors, omissions, or contrary
interpretation of the subject matter herein. Any perceived slights of specific persons, peoples, or
organizations are unintentional. In practical advice books, like anything else in life, there are no
guarantees of income made. Readers are cautioned to reply on their own judgment about their
individual circumstances to act accordingly. This book is not intended for use as a source of legal,
business, accounting or financial advice. All readers are advised to seek services of competent
professionals in legal, business, accounting, and finance field.*

IME Publishing Group. —1st ed.
ISBN: - 978-0-9973034-4-5

Independence Public Adjusters · AZ Lic# 1039385 · CA Lic# 2109693

DEDICATION

TO FIRE VICTIMS everywhere who we hope will benefit from the information provided in this book. May it help them see how insurance claims really work in favor of the insurance company and give them guidance to see through the hype of slick advertising and insurance companies for what they really are.

WHAT OTHERS ARE SAYING ABOUT ANTHONY AND STEVE FROM IPA

After our Church was vandalized, we spent over two months trying to get our insurance company to pay our claim. Within six weeks of hiring Independent Public Adjusters we received a settlement of over 4 times the amount that was originally offered by our insurance company. **Pastor Deborah and Esley Simmon, South Sacramento Christian Center Church**

Not only did they secure for me what was due on the insurance claim; but they exceed my expectation in every way. Tony and Steve are A-1 professionals and awesome individuals; extremely helpful. I can't say good enough for Independent Public Adjuster. It was heaven sent to me. And I could keep on going........and going....... thank you!!!
Helen Burga De Naruse – Business Owner.

I would recommend Independent Public Adjuster to anyone having problems with payment and resolution of insurance claim matters. Only regret I have is that I didn't hire IPA in the beginning. They helped me bring my claim from under $30,000 to over $100,000 in damages. IPA...doing it right! **John Eshelman Prime Mechanical, Livermore, California.**

Tony, I just want to thank you and your team for everything about our house insurance. Me and my wife is very satisfied with everything going on. We know we are still in process but for sure it's going on the right direction. Thank you again. **Sherwin/ Marjorie Family**

Thanks Tony & Company for all your expertise in representing us! You guys are fantastic. Hopefully we will never need you again, but if we do, you're in!!!! **Patrick Addison**

We knew we needed a professional to work on our behalf … In spite of the overbearing competitor and his false statements we chose Tony Astone with IPA . Tony was perfect! Within no time he secured a much, much larger payment for the structure than the insurance going to pay. Then he had a forensic CPA intercede and collect all of our Business interruption payments for a year and a half. We never could have figured the formula for that. The contents portion was on a format of excel that he got the max for the policy for us by hiring additional staff to take us step by step. **Don and Barbara Stutzman, Union Hill Inn LLC**

This is to personally thank you for all the hard work and the excellent results that you achieved for my claim. When I first met with Steve I didn't think that I needed your services. When I met with the insurance adjuster and he started throwing around a ridiculously low number for my fire repairs to my home I knew I was in trouble. Tony took quick action and cleaned up the mess and ultimately got me about $100,000 more than I would have received with the help of IPA. You also did an excellent job on the contents settlement and the service was top notch! **Eddie Peter**

ACKNOWLEDGEMENTS

FIRST AND FOREMOST, WE WOULD like to thank our clients, past and present, who have trusted us to guide them through one of the most difficult times in their lives. Without your belief in our abilities, this book would never have been written.

Second, our deepest gratitude to JR Durflinger, who saw the value of our experience and encouraged us to write a book that showed our expertise in the field of public adjusting.

We must also thank Mike Driggers, without whom this book would never have been completed. Thank you for your dedication and guidance during this process.

Lastly, thank you to our friends and family who have supported our vision over these many years. You know who you are.

TABLE OF CONTENTS

CHAPTER 1

Why We Wrote This Book

IF YOU HAVE SUFFERED A LARGE PROPERTY loss, this book is written for you. It will assist you in understanding the complexities and hurdles you may face during the claims process. People are often misled into thinking that when they have a large property insurance claim, their insurance company will treat them "like a good neighbor." However, every large property claim will end with less money in your pocket if you do not have the help of a public adjuster. Also, hiring a public adjuster will help the homeowner or business owner avoid or steer clear of the land mines that are discussed in this book. The details in this book are very general and cover just a small fraction of the pitfalls, issues and complexities that arise during a large property claim. These chapters give the reader a sneak preview of what can and likely will be experienced down the road when the smoke clears.

Our Background

Tony Astone began working as an insurance adjuster with Safeco Insurance Company in 1991. He immediately handled small property claims and was promoted to the position of general adjuster where he handled large commercial claims throughout the United States. In 1993, Tony joined Kemper National Insurance Company and handled large commercial claims throughout the United States. In 2003, Tony rejoined Safeco Insurance Company as a unit manager for property claims, handling highly technical claims and mold claims. In 2008, Tony decided to make the transition from an insurance adjuster to a public adjuster working on behalf of the client instead of the insurance company. It was a natural fit and in 2012, Tony co-founded Independence Public Adjusters, Inc. with Steve Boydstun, an experienced sales and marketing professional. Steve was licensed in 2012 as a public adjuster in California and Arizona and since that time has hired and manages IPA's public adjusters in the Bay Area, San Joaquin Valley and throughout the Sacramento area He has developed the sales and marketing department for IPA and provides training and support to IPA's staff of public adjusters. Steve also oversees all phases of the Department of Insurance Regulations, DOI testing, and compliance with those regulations.

The Purpose of This Book

We hope this book gives you a better understanding of how property insurance claims work. Most people have never suffered a property or casualty insurance claim. (We are not covering health, life or worker's compensation in this book.) Most of those same people have never read their insurance policy. Even after filing the claim, they have no idea of what the claims process will be, and they rely on the insurance adjuster to walk them through the process. People need to understand what can happen as the claim progresses to ensure that they are not completely at the mercy of the insurance adjuster. The policyholder needs to be paid every dollar they are entitled to and have peace of mind knowing that their claim is being handled correctly. Insurance companies and their claims adjusters rely on the ignorance of their own policyholders.

Policyholders most often do not read and/or do not understand the fine print in their policies. That lack of knowledge can cost them thousands in settlement dollars and, worst of all, their peace of mind. As you read these chapters, we hope you will gain a better understanding of the complex nature of an insurance claim and why hiring a public adjuster is an important part of the claims process.

CHAPTER 2

How Insurance Works

MOST PEOPLE HAVE NEVER READ THEIR insurance policy. Now that you have suffered a major property loss, your policy is activated and working for you, assuming your loss is covered. If you have insurance on your home and belongings, you are about to find out if you "are in good hands" or if your insurance company is "like a good neighbor" or if it is "on your side." When you purchased your insurance policy, most likely you purchased it from your local agent or online. Your agent is the salesman, but now that you have a claim against the insurance company, you will no longer be dealing with your agent, but with your claims adjuster.

How Does an Insurance Company Make Money?

Let's start with a bit of background into the insurance world. It is widely believed that insurance companies make money by taking in more revenue than the amount of money that is paid for claims. This is NOT true. On average, most insurance companies pay one dollar and two cents in claims and expenses for every dollar that they bring in on premiums. How then, does an insurance company make enough revenue to stay in business if they lose two cents for every dollar? By holding on to that dollar for as long as possible, it earns money in investment markets. The pool of money is invested in diversified accounts. The longer the money can stay in the market without being withdrawn to pay claims, the more money it earns in investment markets.

Understanding Reserves

Insurance companies are financially motivated to control and restrict the amount of money leaving the investment pool to pay claims. After a property claim is filed, the claims adjuster must report to management how much he believes it is going to cost the company to settle the claim, which in turn, alerts the company as to how much money to take out of the investment pool to pay the claim. Money that is withdrawn from the investment pool to pay claims is called a *Reserve*. Every three months, the insurance companies must review their actuaries to decide how much money to take out of the investment pool and place into the reserves. The solvency of the insurance company is rated based on its ability to pay claims by comparing loss projections to the cash assets. A very common rating is from an organization called A.M. Best Rating Services. The best rating possible for an insurance company under the A.M. is AAA. The worst rating is a C. If the agency drops or reduces a rating for an insurance company, it can have catastrophic consequences for the reputation, marketing, and future sales for the insurance company. If an insurance company under-reports its reserves, then the financial solvency looks better than it really is because it gives the appearance that they have more money available to pay claims. However, if the insurance company overstates its reserves, then it gives the appearance that the company has less money to pay its claims. The accuracy of the reported reserves is important because it is one of the many elements that is evaluated to determine the rating of the company. Your claims adjuster is under considerable pressure to place a timely and accurate reserve for your claim. The timing and the accuracy of the reserve recommendation will contribute to your adjuster's score on his performance review. This will be discussed in more detail in chapter 3.

What Is The Role of the Adjuster?

Money paid on claims is the largest expense for any insurance company, and the claim adjuster is responsible for determining the amount of money that should be paid to settle the claim. Therefore, the adjuster's decision on the amount to pay a claim has an impact on the bottom line for the insurance company. Most property claim adjusters are hired out of college by the insurance companies. Their training normally starts at the home office where they are trained on procedures, coverage, claim investigation, reserves and construction. They normally start adjusting claims over the phone handling small dollar claims. After a year or so they may get promoted to "field adjuster" where they get a company car and start handling larger claims like pipe leaks, vandalism, and small fire losses.

Within a few years, they may graduate and become a large loss adjuster, who handles large loss claims. They may also be asked to work claims in several states. If you have suffered a large property loss, a low-level adjuster may be deployed to begin the claim investigation. If the estimated value of your claim is above the authority amount of the low-level adjuster, it will likely be transferred to a middle or large loss adjuster. Sometimes a large property claim can be transferred as many as three or four times. This can be frustrating and can waste valuable time.

When you suffer a large property loss, your claim may be assigned to a low or middle-level adjuster. Moreover, when your claim is assigned to an adjuster, you have no input on who they select to handle your claim. In general, the lower and mid-level adjusters are not as reasonable or generous when it comes to paying a claim, unlike a large-level adjuster who is more experienced and used to paying claims in the hundreds of thousands of dollars. Consider this the benefit of hiring a public adjuster at the beginning of your claim is that it will almost certainly be assigned to a large loss adjuster.

The Independent Adjusters

In some instances, an insurance company may not have the resources to assign an *in-house* adjuster to a large property claim, so they assign it to an *Independent Adjuster(IA)*. An IA is an independent contractor who is hired by an insurance company to document a claim and recommend a settlement amount. The advantage of having a claim assigned to an IA is that the IA is not as conditioned by your insurance company to cut corners on your claim since they are not employed or trained by your insurance company. The disadvantage, however, is the IA has no authority and so essentially another moving part to the claim process is resulting in a slower settlement. Ultimately, if your claim is assigned to an IA, chances are they won't be so cheap, but it may take longer to settle your claim.

Conditions In Your Policy You Need To Know

Under the Conditions section of your policy, it specifically states that the insurance company will pay the least amount required to repair or replace your covered property with *Like Kind and Quality*. The decision to "replace" or "repair" can be extremely subjective. For example, if you had a fire in a bedroom and smoke infiltrated the kitchen cabinets, do the cabinets need replacing or can they be cleaned or repaired? As a homeowner, you would likely prefer new cabinets to ensure that they won't smell like smoke after they are cleaned. However, the adjuster would prefer you agree to have the cabinets cleaned and save his company the expense of installing costly new ones. Consider this, even if your adjuster agrees to replace your cabinets, how will you know if they are being replaced with comparable quality materials? For instance, if you have ever had an automobile claim for collision damage to your car, you were likely told by the auto-adjuster that the dollar value of your claim payment would be based on the cost of using after-market automobile parts and not Original Equipment Manufacturer (OEM) parts. Like after-market parts, your large loss homeowner adjuster may try to get away with the same thing when it comes to pricing out materials. This is what they are trained to do. The adjuster's work performance is measured on their ability to show claims management how they saved the company money on the adjustment and settlement of your claim. And all at your expense. The irony of this is that after the claim is settled, many people are satisfied with the outcome. The reason is that the average homeowner does not have the experience and training to understand the true dollar value of their claim. Relying on your claim adjuster to determine the amount of your loss is not in your best interest and is a conflict of interest.

Is The Insurance Agent Your Friend?

Your insurance agent is a salesperson. Their job is to ensure that you have proper coverage and limits in your policy. Most agents do not have the training or experience level of the claims adjuster, although most have enough knowledge about claims to conduct their business. Also, your insurance agent is dependent upon the insurance company for their end-of-

-year bonus. At the end of each year, the insurance company looks at the agent's book of business to compare the amount of premium dollars earned compared to the dollar amount paid out on claims. Simply put, the lower amount paid in claims, the larger the year-end bonus. Therefore, your agent, like your adjuster, would like to see the insurance company minimize the amount of your claim settlement. The lower the amount paid, the better for your agent come bonus time. Your agent has little or no influence on what the insurance company does or does not do. If your agent tells you he or she is "on your side" and can assist you with the claim, don't be fooled. Most agents don't have the experience to be of much help to their clients who have suffered a large property loss. Additionally, if you tell your agent that you have hired or are considering hiring a public adjuster, it is likely that your agent will try to talk you out of this. The reason is two-fold. First, he may believe that you are not relying on him to assist you with your claim. Secondly, your agent knows from experience that when an insured hires a public adjuster, the amount of the settlement will increase 20% to 45% on average. The more the insurance company pays on your agent's book of business, the lower the bonus at the end of the year. Therefore, in general, agents prefer their customers not use public adjusters. Surprisingly, it is a fact that the insurance company writes a policy that is hard to understand, so wouldn't it be fair to say that a credible agent would recommend you hire a public adjuster to help maximize your claim?

CHAPTER 3

What Are Public Adjusters?

A PUBLIC ADJUSTER IS AN ADVOCATE FOR the insured. The role of the public adjuster is to process, present and negotiate the property insurance claim on behalf of the insured. Most public adjusters are required to be licensed by the Department of Insurance in the state for which they conduct their business. Many public adjusters are licensed in multiple states. Most states have professional associations for public adjusters. For example, in the State of California, it is CAPIA, the California Association of public adjusters. There is also a national association called NAPIA, the National Association of Public Insurance Adjusters. These associations provide a professional forum for the public adjuster to share new information, rules, regulations, and to also police one another. There are laws and rules of ethics within the Department of Insurance regulations that public adjusters are required to abide by. Any public adjuster who intentionally goes outside any of the rules or regulations may create a competitive advantage against industry competition. Therefore, as a professional community, public adjusters often monitor one another by what they see and hear in the field.

Why The History About Public Adjusters Matters.

The history of the first recorded public adjusters goes back as far as 1880. Back then, the first public adjusters were described as a new and disorganized group of professionals that had little training, standards of ethics, or rules or regulations to follow. Today, there are thousands of licensed public adjusters found in most states, with Texas having more than 10,000 licensed public adjusters alone. While this may sound like the profession is booming, the fact is that most people have never heard of a public adjuster.

Because the profession of public adjusting is widely unknown among the public and because their services apply to such a small percentage of the population who may suffer a major property loss, it is not cost-effective to market the services using mainstream media such as newspapers or TV advertisements. Additionally, it is difficult for public adjusters to advertise to a specific market. Consequently, the best way a public adjuster can market to someone who may need the service is to meet with the insured "after" the event that caused the property loss. This necessity is the unpleasant side of the business for two reasons. First, there is the perception that public adjusters are "Firetruck Chasers." The reality is that the public adjuster's only way to promote their service is to meet with the insured soon after the event. They will need to introduce them to the profession and educate them about the value of the service. Often, this type of solicitation is not well received by the insured who may be under stress after suffering a major property loss. Secondly, the aggressive approach by some public adjusters is to get the home or business owner to sign a contract for his service. While there are rules and regulations outlined by the Department of Insurance which establish guidelines on solicitation, there are no hard and fast rules in place to address ethics or individual behavior. In general, public adjusters are there with good intentions and thanks to professional associations like NAPIA and CAPIA, the bad behavior of overly aggressive or corrupt public adjusters is in decline and their reputation and usefulness is much more accepted and understood.

Today the profession of Public Adjusting is relatively standardized. Strict laws and regulations by the Department of Insurance as well as professional associations like NAPIA and CAPIA, keep a close eye on licensing and continuing education for all public adjusters. However, public adjusting Firms and individuals are anything but standardized. Like any other service-based business, the profession/business of public adjusters offers a wide range of companies and individuals to choose from. For the most part, there seems to be two types of Public Adjusting Companies the consumer must choose from. For example, in the State of California there seems to be either large companies or small companies to choose from. Let's look at the make-up and the pros and cons of each type of firm.

Why Choosing the Right Firm Is Important.

The large Public Adjusting Firms tend to have multiple offices throughout the state and even throughout the country. In general, the larger firms run their organization like a large corporation in terms of segregated departments. They usually have licensed public adjusters who are in sales or in claims. Anyone who represents themselves as a public adjuster must be licensed in that State. A public adjuster who works for a large firm in sales is truly a licensed public adjuster, but chances are their main objective is to get the insured to sign the contract and it is likely that the salesperson has never actually adjusted a claim before. After a large fire, the large firm will send a salesperson to the location of the property loss. The salesperson for the larger firm likely has fancy and expensive marketing material like brochures, hand-outs or websites. Once the salesperson gets the insured to sign the contract, the claim is turned over to a separate public adjuster in the same firm who handles the claim. The large firms may be sensitive to the perception, especially considering the bad reputation of public adjusters, mostly in the past, that the insured may feel like there is a bit of bait and switch when the insured signs with the saleperson and then the claim gets turned over to the claim technician. Some firms may create the deception that the salesperson is actually a President or Vice President to create the illusion that he/she is not "just a salesperson." There is nothing wrong with the practice of sale and turn-over as long as the roles are honestly explained to the insured. The insured should be getting an honest and knowledgeable public adjuster who, at the end of the day, is going to advocate and provide a valuable service to the insured. The large firms tend to have larger overhead and, as a result, they may not be as competitive as the smaller firms with pricing. The larger firms also tend to have more internal politics and bureaucracy that their adjusters must deal with. This may result in the adjuster having less authority and autonomy in handling your claim. The larger firms are financially tailored to handling larger claims with a higher concentration of commercial claims that are usually more than $300,000.

Regardless of the size of the firm, the most important thing is that the insured is getting a good, honest and knowledgeable public adjuster to handle the insurance claim. The personality, credentials, and technical expertise of the individual public adjuster handling your claim should be more important than the size or reputation of the firm. Smaller public adjusting firms usually have only one or more offices in the same state. The smaller firms may be as small as a one-man shop or may have less than ten people in the organization. The person pitching the sale may be the same person handling your claim. Or, the smaller firm may use the salesperson and separate adjuster model that the larger firms tend to use or a hybrid version. Because the smaller firms generally have less overhead due to fewer offices, fewer employees and less expensive marketing tools, they tend to be more competitive in pricing. These firms predominately handle mostly homeowner and smaller commercial losses below $300,000. However, please do not take from this that the smaller firms are not as proficient as the larger firms to handle larger homeowner or commercial claims. The reality is that the larger firms have better sales resources, and by nature of their size and access to capital, they are better able to compete with the smaller firms on the sales side of larger claims. The theory of evolution applies to any business the same as it does to the profession of public adjusting. The larger fish tend to eat the smaller fish. It is the perception that the larger firms intentionally create in their marketing that they are superior over the smaller firms because of their prestige, superior business acumen, and sharp shooter salespeople. The truth of the matter is that the experience, knowledge, personality, and background of the individual public adjuster and his or her team that is going to actually handle the claim is by far more important than the image created by the larger firms that they are the elite. Therefore, it is important to ask anyone soliciting you as a public adjuster one very simple question before you decide which firm to hire: **Who is the actual public adjuster(s) who is going to handle my claim from start to finish and when can I interview him or her?** The actual public adjuster who is going to handle your claim should be the person that you get to know, before you decide to hire.

Do not be fooled by all the fancy marketing materials and/or the self-created perception of the larger firms that they are superior to the smaller firms. As noted, consideration of who the actual public adjuster is that is going to handle your claim is more important than the image of the firm. Like any other profession, there are good and bad public adjusters. The best way to cut through the sales pitch and the marketing material is to sit down with your public adjuster and interview them. The background education and professional experience are the most important things to consider when hiring a public adjuster or their firm. Some things to consider with regards to the background is whether the public adjuster has ever worked as a claims adjuster for an insurance company. As they say, the best way to beat the enemy may be to know the enemy. Also, make sure that you ask for referrals of prior clients, get their phone numbers and call them for their opinions. Interviewing honest referrals is one of the best ways to determine if the public adjuster can walk the walk instead of just talking the talk. It also does not hurt to go on the firm's website to obtain important information about the organization and the culture. Lastly, go to your state Department of Insurance to see if there have been any violations or complaints filed against them. Once you have decided which firm to hire, it is important to understand what the role and goal of the public adjuster should be. The public adjuster should principally accomplish two important objectives for the insured. First, the public adjusterhandles all meetings, preparation and paper work of the claim so that the insured does not have to. This is an important aspect of the service which allows the insured to live their life with fewer disruptions than if they try to handle the claim themselves. Secondly, hiring a public adjuster will result in a higher settlement of 20% to 40% on average. A good public adjuster should be able to prove this statistic to you using the outcome of the claims they have handled for their clients. Now that you have some general information about the public adjusting firms and the public adjusting profession, let's see how hiring a public adjuster can save you a lot of headaches and establish a higher settlement.

CHAPTER 4

The Misconception of The Coverage and Claim Investigation

MANY PEOPLE BELIEVE THAT WHEN they have suffered property damage to their home or business, the claim is automatically covered as long as the premium has been paid. This is a huge misconception. Your policy contains many exclusions, limitations and conditions that can cause a claim to be denied or reduced in the amount paid. The intent of this chapter is to give you a basic understanding of how coverage can affect your recovery and how and what you say could cause your claim to be denied or drastically limited in the amount of the recovery.

Your insurance policy is a contract between you and your insurance company. The policy defines you as the *insured* and the insurance company as the *insurer*. The policy is a *contract of adhesion* meaning that it was written by only one party to the contract. In this case, it was written by the insurer. Despite all the pages, sections, and technical wording in your policy, there are times when the wording does not address the specific situation (peril) that caused the property loss or the wording is ambiguous. Court cases show that if the policy does not adequately address the situation of the claim or if the wording is ambiguous, the courts generally rule in favor of the insured because the policy is a contract of adhesion and the insurer had the opportunity to get the policy right when they wrote it. This is a very general way of saying that since your insurance company wrote the policy without your input, if the policy is vague or ambiguous, then you (the insured) should get the benefit of the doubt and not the insurer. This concept makes coverage determination one of the most interesting and subjective aspects of an insurance claim. This accounts for hundreds of case laws from state to state that can be used to gauge the outcome of a coverage determination. Unfortunately, the insurer gets to interpret the policy and make the coverage determination and not you. There are hundreds of lawsuits filed each year by insureds who are suing their insurer for bad faith under the contention that the insurer failed to properly interpret their own contract and erroneously or intentionally denied the claim accordingly.

The Differences Between Homeowner and Commercial Policies

There are basically two parts to any Homeowner or Commercial property insurance policy. The first part is called the Declarations. The policy Declaration pages show the inception dates of the policy, the named insured, and the property address covered under the policy. It also shows all the forms and endorsements that go with the policy in addition to the dollar limits for the Structure, Contents, and the Additional Living Expenses(ALE). One of the first things that your insurance adjuster will do after the claim has been filed is to review the Declaration pages for coverage confirmation. This portion of the claim investigation is relatively cut and dry. However, coverage issues involving the Declarations can and do come into play. For example, suppose you inherited a home from your deceased parents, and the home is insured under the name of your parents and it catches on fire before you had the policy transferred into your name? Will the insurance company deny the claim because the insureds are deceased? Can you go back and amend the policy to list yourself as the insured? Suppose that your policy expires on June 15, 2017 and that on June 14, 2017, you disposed of ashes from your BBQ. The ashes smoldered for two days and then caused a fire that started on June 16, 2017. Did the claim fall inside or outside the coverage period? These are just a few of the examples of how coverage issues can come into play regarding the Declaration pages of the policy.

The second part of the standard Homeowner and Commercial property policy is the Coverage Form(s). Most of these policies are standardized by the Insurance Services Office (ISO). The other alternative is that the insurer can write their own custom policy which may offer broader coverage. Regardless of whether your policy is an ISO form or written specifically by your insurer, the Coverage Form addresses the three basic types of coverages under most policies which are:

1) Dwelling/Structure;
2) Personal Belongings/Contents; and
3) Additional Living Expenses (ALE) or Business Income Loss.

The coverage form also lists the Definitions, Exclusions, Limitations and Conditions that apply to the Dwelling, Contents and ALE coverage. Insurance policies contain dozens of exclusions and conditions that are specified in hard to read fine print and unusual wording. Paragraphs that provide or define coverage in one part of the policy may be amended in other paragraphs that completely change the coverage or definition. As noted earlier, the policy language in the Coverage Form can be vague and/or ambiguous. For example, if the policy excludes damage to the Dwelling caused by rodents and a mouse chewed thru an electrical wire that caused a fire, is the damage from the fire covered? The answer to this question could determine if the claim is covered (paid) or excluded (denied). When one event (the mouse) triggers another event (fire), this is called *concurrent causation*. How does your policy react to this? The wording in the coverage form can also limit the dollar amount of your recovery. For example, most standard Homeowners policies have a limit of $2500 for any personal property that was used for business purposes. If you are a plumber and you retired ten years ago, what happens if a fire destroys $20,000 of your tools stored in your garage? The standard policy contains a Condition that requires the insured to report the claim in a "reasonable" amount of time. Suppose that you knew of a slow pipe leak that caused a small water stain on your carpet and when you returned from vacation three days later, the volume of water from the leak increased and caused substantial water damage throughout the flooring in your home. Can the insurance company deny your claim because you failed to report the claim when you first noticed the leak?

The examples above involving coverage determination are intentionally small and easy to understand to make a point. Most large property claims involve coverage issues that are much more complex. There are many different policy Exclusions, Limitations and Conditions that will apply to your claim. The situation of your claim in relation to the policy language will be interpreted by your adjuster, who is motivated to shave the dollars of your claim recovery if given the opportunity. Anything that you say can and will be held against you. I would encourage you to find your property policy and read it before you say anything to the insurer that will negatively affect the outcome of your claim. Better yet, find your policy and have a licensed public adjuster review it for you for a coverage opinion.

In addition to the Coverage Forms, most Homeowner and Commercial property policies also come with other forms and endorsements that either enhance or restrict the coverage outlined on the Coverage Form. One of the most common endorsements under the Homeowner and Commercial property policy is for *Code Upgrades*. The standard Coverage forms either do not cover Code Upgrades or limit the recovery by 5% or 10% of the limit for the structure. Most policies have several endorsements that customize the policy coverage to fit the needs of the insured. Your agent or broker is responsible for making sure that your policy (including endorsements) will fully compensate you in the event you suffer a covered property loss. Often, the endorsements override or supersede the coverage outlined in the main Coverage Form. Sometimes even the endorsements have provisions that override or supersede each other. Reading a policy with many endorsements is like reading a road map. It is full of complicated twists and turns, fine print, and unusual wording. Hopefully, if you have suffered a large property loss, your agent or broker has customized your policy with various endorsements that will completely cover you in the event of an unexpected catastrophe.

What Is Actual Cash Value vs. Replacement Cost?

Most property policies have a section under the Conditions section that spells out how a claim is to be paid out in the event of a covered claim. Without going into detail of how and why this works, most policies pay the *Actual Cash Value* of the claim. This means that for certain items that normally depreciate over time, the policy applies a dollar amount of depreciation that is subtracted from the *Replacement Cost* in order to make the Actual Cash Value payment. Most Homeowner and Commercial policies pay the Actual Cash Value at first and then pay the Replacement Cost only after an item has been replaced. For example, if you are making a claim for damaged carpet and the carpet was 3 years old at the time of the loss, the insurance adjuster is going to apply a calculated rate of depreciation based on the age and condition of the carpet at the time of the loss. If the rate of depreciation is calculated to be 25% and the Replacement Cost of the carpet is $1000, then the insurer is going to subtract $250 of depreciation from the Replacement Cost and issue an Actual Cash Value payment of $750. Most policies pay the Replacement Cost and refund the amount of depreciation withheld when the insured incurs the cost to replace the property. This applies to damage to the dwelling and your personal belongings. So, in this example, if the insured spends only $900 to replace the carpet, the insurer will refund the insured $150 of the $250 that was withheld. What happens if the actual cost of the carpet is $1250? It is an obvious conflict of your best interest to stand idle and let your insurance company decide the amount of the Replacement Cost and/or Depreciation.

The Claim Investigation Process

All property insurance policies contain an exclusion for any loss intentionally caused by the insured. Moreover, every year there are millions of dollars of insurance claims paid and denied caused by insurance fraud. Fraud comes in two forms:

1. An intentional act caused by the insured to collect insurance proceeds.
2. Inflating the amount of a claim that was not the result of an intentional act.

If the insurer suspects that you or a family member intentionally caused a property loss or that you are trying to inflate the amount of the recovery, then your claim will likely be transferred to the *Special Investigative Unit (SIU)*. The SIU department is the equivalent of the insurance investigation department. It is staffed by investigators that are highly trained to investigate suspicious fraud claims. Many of the SIU employees are retired police officers. The SIU investigator will tell you that their position is to rule you out so that the claim can be paid. They may act like your best friend to get you to open up. Their job performance is determined by the number of claims they can influence to get denied or reduced. It is not cheap for the insurer to finance the SIU department, so it is imperative that the Department justifies its existence by saving the insurance company more than they cost, which is why the SIU investigator is on a mission to make a case for fraud at every given opportunity. The conclusion that a claim involves fraud can be subjective, and when an SIU agent classifies a large property claim as fraudulent, the impact to an innocent insured can be devastating.

Most claims that get referred to SIU are not fraudulent, but they look suspicious for one reason or another. Claims adjusters are trained to identify "Red Flags" such as arson. Arson fires are probably the most common form of property fraud claims. Other common forms of fraud are theft claims. However, the most common types of fraud claims are those that are intentionally inflated. Therefore, the SIU investigator is looking for motive and the opportunity for the insured to commit the fraudulent act. Unfortunately, fraud does happen, people do get caught, and it costs most insurance companies millions of dollars a year in fraudulent claim payments. For this reason, the insurance company tends to take the position that if you file a large property claim, you are guilty of fraud until proven innocent. Most insureds who have a large property claim are under the microscope of the insurance company. Your claim history, employment status, finances, credit history, bank records, bankruptcies, and court records will be considered by SIU as part of their investigation.

Examination Under Oath Participation

Another part of the SIU Investigation involves the insured being required to participate in an *Examination Under Oath (EUO)*. The requirement of the EUO is specified under the Conditions section of the policy. If required by the insurer, the insured is obligated to participate in the EUO, and failure to participate could and likely would result in the entire claim being denied. Under the EUO, the insurer hires an attorney to take the testimony of the insured under penalty of perjury. After the EUO, the attorney for the insurer will give an opinion as to whether the claim should be paid or denied. An insured would be encouraged to hire his own attorney for the EUO. An EUO can be very costly for the insured, and it usually delays the outcome or payment of the claim for about 3 months on average. Most claims that go to an EUO are eventually covered and paid. The amount of expense, delays, and stress that the EUO process can cause to an insured is very unfortunate and many times can be avoided if the insured has an advocate in their corner during the claims investigation.

The Negotiated Settlement Game

The end result of SIU involvement or the EUO process might be that the insurer feels the decision to deny or pay the claim lies within the gray area of the policy. In this case, the insurer may want to settle the claim instead of taking the risk of denying it and the possibility of being sued. If the insured feels that the claim coverage falls in the gray area, then instead of just paying the entire amount of the claim, they may try to get some mileage out of the situation. The insurer may convince the insured that they should take less than what was claimed as a compromise opposed to the claim being denied. The result of this agreement between the insured and the insurer will be a *negotiated settlement.* Usually, the insurer and the insured will agree to sign a document called a *White vs Western waiver.* (White vs. Western Title Insurance Company 1995 40 Cal .3d 870) first used this type of an agreement during the negotiations that ultimately failed. A *White vs Western* waiver is an agreement stating that when two parties are negotiating a claim, nothing said or disclaimed during the negotiation discussions can be allowed in the discovery of any litigation. This means that anything either party says or any documentation produced during the negotiations is off the record. This does not make its way into the claim file and cannot legally be brought into any form of litigation. If the claim ends up being settled through the negotiations, the insurer will likely require the insured to sign a document called a *policyholder's release,* meaning that both parties agree the amount of the settlement is full and final, and neither party can file suit against the other. If you find that your claim is entering into a negotiated settlement, you need to know the strengths and weaknesses of your case in order to decide how much, if any, you should be willing to compromise. You need someone on your side who has the experience and knowledge to articulate the merits of your case or weaknesses in preparation for the negotiations. You also need someone in your corner that may be able to recognize the opportunity of a negotiated settlement that will benefit you more than harm you. For example, if you negotiate a settlement, you might be able to get Replacement Cost without depreciation which will benefit you. Having an expert on your side will also allow you to articulate and back up the errors or bad faith potentially committed by the insurer that will strengthen your position. Lastly, in the event that the claim cannot be settled through negotiations, you need someone to help you decide what the next step is someone who will know the strengths and weaknesses of both sides and prepare a cost-benefit analysis to help decide what action who will, if any, you should take against the insurer. It is worth noting that only five percent of all large property claims end up going to a negotiated settlement and roughly 90% end up settling. Just like a covered claim, you need an expert with you to avoid leaving any money on the table when you negotiate the settlement. The insurer will be prepared to pay you the least amount possible to make the claim go away without litigation.

Let Me Explain What Waiver, Estoppel and Detrimental Reliance is

By now you might be able to clearly see how complicated a coverage investigation can be based on the circumstances of the claim in relation to the policy language and coverage afforded under the policy. Since claims adjusters and insurance company employees are humans, mistakes can and do happen. An adjuster is allowed to make a mistake and change direction or retract his or her original position, but only if the insured has not financially relied on the incorrect representation made by the adjuster. For instance, let's say that the insurance adjuster tells you that that his company is going to cover the cost to replace your hardwood flooring due to damage from a paint spill. Two days later, and before you financially commit to the repairs, the adjuster informs you that they are denying the claim, because they determined that your dog caused the paint to spill and there is a policy exclusion for damage caused by pets. Even though the adjuster first stated that the claim was covered, they can retract their position and deny the claim if you did not financially act or commit to the mistake that the claim was covered.

Using the scenario above, say that after the adjuster told you that the claim was covered, you entered into a contract to have the flooring replaced and you paid half the cost as a deposit. The fact that you have financially committed to the repairs based upon the adjuster's representation that your claim was covered prevents the adjuster from denying your claim two days later when it was determined that the paint spill was caused by your dog. This is an example of *waiver, estoppel and detrimental reliance.* Your down payment and contractual obligation to pay to have the flooring replaced is considered a financial reliance based upon the representation of the insurer that the claim is covered. This financial reliance becomes a *detrimental reliance* if the insurer then denies the claim. If the adjuster realizes the mistake to cover the loss and there has been detrimental reliance on behalf of the insured, then courts have ruled that the insurer has waived (*waiver*) their rights to enforce the applicable policy provision(s). The insurer is also "*estopped*" from asserting the applicable policy exclusion or limitation in order to deny or limit the recovery. If your insurance adjuster commits to coverage and you financially spend or commit to the cost or repairs or replacement, then by law, the insurer has breached the right to deny or limit the claim. Although this situation is rare, the fact is that it does happen on occasion and having an advocate in your corner is important to inform you of your rights under the policy and in law.

You're On Notice - Reservation of Rights Letter

When an insurer is aware of a potential coverage issue that arises during the claim investigation, the insurer will usually send the insured a letter called a Reservation of Rights (ROR). The ROR letter is intended to place the insured on notice of the specific coverage issue that exists and advises the insured that the insured is not to misconstrue the claim investigation as a commitment of coverage during the claim investigation. The letter also reserves the rights of the insurered. It applies or enforces any policy language that may apply at any time during the investigation including their right to require an EUO or to even allow the insurer to deny or limit the claim. If you understood the paragraph above regarding detrimental reliance, waiver and estoppel, then you can see that the purpose of the ROR letter is to avoid this. The ROR letter is a self-serving letter for the insurer to cover their mistake in an effort to avoid the waiver and estoppel issues in the event that the insured misinterprets the claim investigation as a commitment to coverage. The decision for an insurer to send an ROR letter is discretionary, and the carrier may send an ROR based on even the slightest chance of a coverage issue. The ROR letter can cause unnecessary stress on the insured since most claims investigated under an ROR letter are ultimately covered.

In most instances, the result of a large property claim is that the insured is either happy or not happy with the outcome. The following are three basic reasons why the insured may not be happy with the outcome of the claim:

1. The claim was paid to the insured's satisfaction, but the process to get to the payment was unpleasant.
2. The claim was paid, but the insured was not happy with the amount paid.
3. The claim was not paid because the insurer deemed there was no coverage and the claim was denied.

If you have suffered a large property claim, be prepared to be frustrated by the claim process. You can expect long meetings with the adjuster(s), being interviewed or being required to take a recorded statement or participate in an EUO. Also, you may be required to sign a background authorization so that your insurance company may check your employment, salary, and credit history. You may have to deal with an adjuster and an SIU Investigator at the same time. You may end up with a claim settled with a cryptic looking computer estimate that makes no sense to you because your adjuster is not taking the time to explain it to you. You may be required to complete your own inventory for your total loss contents inside your home that may be dangerous, full of smoke and contain asbestos. Your adjuster might tell you something can be repaired when you know that it should be replaced. Also, many find that when you have questions, the adjuster who started out as a caring, attentive advocate, now rarely answers the phone or is slow to return your calls. Contrary to all the public relation advertisements, it is highly likely that when you are dealing with your insurance company involving a large property claim, you will not be treated like a good neighbor, you will not be in good hands, and your insurance company will not be on your side. At the beginning of the claims process, it is suggested that you journalize every discussion you have with everyone representing your insurance company.

What Is The Appraisal Process?

When an insured has a dispute regarding the amount paid under the claim, the dispute can be resolved through a process called *Appraisal.* The process of the appraisal is found in the Conditions section of your policy. The insured and the insurer each hire their own appraiser (at their own expense) to collect the information and rule on the dollar amount of the loss. If the appraisers cannot agree to the loss amount, then the ruling goes to an umpire who makes the ultimate decision. The cost of the umpire is split between the insured and the insurer. The appraisal process can be expensive and it can delay the resolution of the claim for months. It is usually not worth the expense and time if the dispute is less than $10,000. The insurer is bound by the outcome of the appraisal and is obligated to pay the amount of the judgment to the insured. If the insured is not happy with the judgment, then the time and expense may not have been worth it, so the appraisal process can be risky. The appraisal provision only deals with disputes involving the dollar amount of the damages. It cannot be used to dispute coverage.

My Claim Was Denied, What Happens Next?

When a claim is denied, it is either properly denied or improperly denied. When it comes to the decision to either pay or deny the claim, your insurance company is the judge and the jury, and you have no say in the decision. As you may know, the fine print of an insurance policy may not adequately address a specific situation. Moreover, the policy language may be ambiguous regarding how the policy should respond to the situation. The result is that insurance companies sometimes deny claims that should be covered, and litigation is the only way to contest the denial of a claim. If the insured files a lawsuit against the insurance company, the insured will seek financial remedy for the physical damages and maybe even punitive damages. Punitive damages are awarded by the courts when they rule that the Insurance company committed the act of *Bad Faith*. The general definition of Bad Faith is *the unreasonable denial of a benefit owed under the contract/policy*. The word "unreasonable" is very subjective and makes the element of Bad Faith very interesting in a court of law. If the courts rule against the insurer for Bad Faith, the insurer may be required to pay up to nine times the amount of the physical damage as punitive damages. The jurisdictions of the courts change from state to state.

In many instances, an insured will experience bad customer service and will not be happy with the amount paid or the claim binge denied. During the claim "process," you cannot file a lawsuit against your insurance company. We live in a litigious society and when we don't get our way, we often threaten with a law suit. Well, your insurance company put some thought into this when they wrote the policy. Within the Conditions section of your policy, there is a provision called the *"No Suit Against Us."* This provision of every policy specifies that the insured cannot sue the insurer unless there has been compliance with the policy provisions. As mentioned above, the appraisal clause is a provision of the policy. Also, under the Conditions section of the policy, there is a provision that specifies that the insured has The Duty to Cooperate with the insurer during the investigation. This means that if you are not happy with customer service, the time it takes, the attitude of your adjuster, the offers being made, or the insurer's decision to send you an ROR or take your EUO, you cannot litigate against your insurance company until you have either invoked the Appraisal clause or the insurer has either paid or denied your claim. Therefore, if you try to litigate your claim during the claim "investigation," the courts will likely suspend the suit based on the No Suit Against Us provision of the policy.

All insurance companies are regulated by the State Department of Insurance (DOI). If an insured is not happy with the insurer during the claim investigation or if an insured is not happy with the outcome of the claim, the insured can file a complaint with the DOI. Unfortunately, most departments are underfunded and understaffed. Even though most departments have made it easier to file complaints with online services, most complaints do not end favorably for the insured. Nevertheless, threatening your insurance company with a DOI complaint may get you some mileage, and it is possible that filing a complaint may result in a favorable outcome.

Reserves

As was mentioned in Chapter 1, your insurance company is under pressure to report timely and accurate reserves. Recommending the amount of the reserve for your claim will be one of the first things required by your insurance adjuster. During the claim investigation, it is your adjuster's job to evaluate the damages and make the reserve recommendation to management. Once the reserve has been set, the adjuster is motivated to settle the claim with an amount as close as possible to the reserve. This means that if your adjuster makes a mistake and under reserves your claim, he is going to do whatever we can to get the claim settled for the lowest amount possible to minimize the discrepancy against the low reserve. **If you hire a public adjuster in the beginning of the claim investigation, your insurance adjuster is likely going to set a higher reserve because he knows that the public adjuster will increase the amount of the settlement.** If you wait to hire a public adjuster and the insurance adjuster has already set the reserve, then the insurance adjuster is going to go out of his way to defend and settle the claim within the amount of the low reserve. In other words, the insurance adjuster does not want to go back to management after you hire a public adjuster to ask for a higher reserve. Therefore, when an insured believes they should wait to get an offer from their insurance adjuster before they hire a public adjuster, in all likelihood this will be a big mistake.

This chapter is just a very general and brief illustration of what you can expect from your insurance company when you are dealing with a large property claim. When you have a large property claim, you are considered a nuisance by your insurance company. You do not get to pick your adjuster and you have no say in the coverage determination or the claim investigation. If you try to handle your claim by yourself, you may experience poor customer service, long interviews and meetings with the adjuster, dealing with fine print policy exclusions. You may also have to deal with limitations including tricky endorsements, SIU, Reservation of Rights letters, Examination Under Oath, suppressed Replacement Cost figures, excessive amounts of Depreciation, a Negotiated Settlement, Appraisal, or have your claim be improperly reduced or denied. If you try to handle your claim without a professional advocate you will be lucky if your claim gets settled to your satisfaction. Chances are, even if you think you have received a good settlement, it is likely you did not receive your maximum recovery. So, if you find yourself going down an unfamiliar road full of intimidating twists and turns, you may find that the decision to handle your claim on your own caused your claim to be unfairly reduced or denied. On the other hand, if you bring in a professional when things go upside down, it may be too late to change the course of your claim! Even if the mistakes you made can be undone by a public adjuster, waiting to hire one when things go downhill can cost you time and money. However, having a public adjuster involved in your claim from the start of your claim can keep you out of trouble. Moreover, it will increase your settlement by 20% to 40% on average.

CHAPTER 5

Dwelling & Structure Claims You Should Understand

I
F YOU HAVE EXPERIENCED A LARGE PROPRTY loss to either your home or your building, and you have an insurance policy in force and proper coverage, your insurance policy is going to contain this standard policy provision stated in the Conditions section of the policy.

"We will pay the cost to _repair_ or _replace_ with similar construction and for the same use on the premises shown in the Declarations."

The determination of whether a component of a structure can be repaired or should be replaced is very subjective and provides the insurance adjuster with the greatest opportunity to cut corners in an effort to save the insurance company money. Adjusters are trained to find ways to repair structural components of a home or building which costs less than replacing them. The adjuster is going to make this determination which is an inherent conflict of interest. Not only is the adjuster trained to find ways to save the insurance company money by repairing instead of replacing, he or she is likely going to bring in professional vendors who will go out of their way to give the opinion that an item can be repaired instead of replaced. If you do not know how to defend yourself from this, chances are it is going to cost you money. Let me share with you a true story that illustrates how this works behind the closed doors of the insurance company office:

In 1992, as an entry level property adjuster working for one of the major insurance companies that is still in business today and thriving, a homeowner claim was assigned to me in San Ramon, CA. It involved an ember that popped out of a fireplace and caused three large burn holes on the family room carpet. The blue carpet, which was about six years old, was wall to wall on the first and second floors of the home, including all the bedrooms. Although I wanted to try to patch the holes, I knew that I would not be able to get away with it because the patches would not match the old carpet and in addition, the homeowner told me he would not accept a "patch job." After completing my estimate to remove and replace the carpet throughout the entire house which came to around $6500, my claim file, which included photos of the damage, a diagram, my estimate, a written coverage analysis and my payment request was placed on the supervisor's desk for his review and approval of the payment. It came to $6000 after subtracting the $500 deductible. My supervisor abruptly called me into his cubicle less than two hours after I placed the file on his desk. He asked me why I was requesting a payment to replace all the carpet. After I explained that it couldn't be adequately patched, he told me to go back to my cubicle, fire up my computer and complete a new estimate to cut the portion of carpet out in front of the fireplace hearth were the burns were, install a new marble hearth and mantel, and then discuss the claim with him. The new estimate totaled $975. After he reviewed the new estimate, he told me to call the insured and "sell" the settlement and offer to waive the $500 deductible. I called my customer and sold the idea an later that day cut a check to the insured for $975 later the insured <u>thanked</u> me.

The example above precisely defines and illustrates what is wrong with the insurance industry. Insurance companies will usually not offer to pay what is owed and will go to great lengths and expense to reduce claim settlements.

Valued Engineering Equals Low Cost Repairs

The previous story is an example of what is referred to as *Valued Engineering*. Valued Engineering is when an adjuster comes up with a way to avoid replacing something by engineering a plan to repair it at a lower cost. Take for example a rafter that has been burned after a fire. A rafter is part of the wood framing of a roof system. It is usually constructed with a 2"x6" wooden stud. If it gets partially burned in a fire, it should be replaced which means that the roof decking attached to the rafter also must be removed and replaced to accommodate the repair. Since the decking must come off, so most the shingles attached to the decking. If the new shingles don't match the existing ones, then all the shingles on the roof must be replaced. As you might imagine, this can become a very expensive repair which may cost around $10,000. The adjuster may decide to hire a structural engineer for $750 who will provide a written opinion and plans showing that the rafter can be repaired by a process called *Sistering,* which means that the burned portion of the rafter will be cut out and two 2"x 6" boards will be bolted into both sides of the rafter to sandwich the portion which has been removed. This may take a carpenter two hours of labor totaling $300, plus $60 for the materials, and $750 for the services of the engineer, for a total cost of $1110. Thanks to Valued Engineering, the claim was settled for $1110 instead of $10,000. The result is that the insured would be stuck with a low-ball settlement and to add insult to injury, the insured may be happy with the settlement. Furthermore, the insured is left with a rafter that looks terrible and if it is noticed in a pre-sale realestate inspection, it could diminish the value of the home or alert the prospective buyer to the situation which could deter the sale of the home. Lastly, being stuck with a sistered rafter is not what the insured had before the fire. Be aware of Valued Engineering and don't let it happen to you on your insurance claim.

Moving the Money

The illustrations above involving the carpet and the rafter happen more than you may think. By having a public adjuster involved early in a claim puts the insured on a level playing field with the insurance company. This ensures that the insured will receive what is owed and not a penny less. Using the carpet scenario, an insured should have been paid $6000 for the claim, but by allowing the insurance company to administer valued engendering (give rise to) the settlement amount was drastically reduced. As an insured, you have the right to choose valued engineering for the repairs and use the rest of the money for other things. However, most people are unaware of this, but the same opportunities that exist for insurance companies to save money (valued engineering) are the same opportunities available to the insured to "move the money" around. Using the carpet example, the insured should have received a settlement of $6000 and could have actually spent $975 to cut out the carpet and remodel the fireplace. If the insured elects to repair the damage with valued engineering and use the rest of the money to do other things, then the cost of the decision is transferred to the insured who is left with a valued engineered repair. The bottom line is that your insurance company owes you to put your home or building back to its pre-loss condition and the application of Valued Engineering might not accomplish this. Realizing you didn't make the claim for purposes of profit, some opportunities that exist to save the insurance company money are the same opportunities that could benefit you instead of the insurance company.

An Important Insurance Industry Tool You Should Know About

A dwelling estimate consists of the scope and repair costs. The scope defines what is being done to repair the structure. For example, remove and replace the front entry door. The cost is the amount of money it will cost for the material and labor to install the door. The Insurance industry uses a software program called *Xactimate* which is the industry leading replacement cost estimating software for property claims adjusters to complete dwelling repair estimates. The estimator starts by completing a "sketch" of the structure. The sketch is the diagram of the floor plan that outlines the dimensions of all the walls, framing and roof angles (hips & valleys). The sketch is required so that the program can determine the quantity of materials to use in the scope. For example, painting the interior of the kitchen walls and ceiling may require 450 square feet of paint, based on the dimensions of the sketch. Once the sketch is completed, the estimator inputs the scope of the interior of the rooms as well as the exterior elevations. The program relies on time studies to determine the amount of labor for each element of the scope. The labor rate is determined by the geographical location of the loss based on the zip code which is then entered into the program. The material costs are based on figures from market prices in the geographical area of the loss. The Xactimate program is updated roughly every three to six months as prices of labor and materials fluctuate. The result of an estimate completed on Xactimate for a large property loss is usually over a hundred pages of cryptic codes and words that are not easy to understand by anyone who has not been trained to use the program. If the insurance adjuster inserts valued engineering into the scope, it would be very unlikely that the average insured would not be able to find it. Below is a sample of a page of a typical Xactimate estimate.

Independence Public Adjusters

5183 Lone Tree Way
Antioch, CA 94531

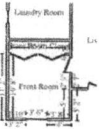

324_BELL

Main Level

Front Room   Height: 8'

241.95 SF Walls	106.84 SF Ceiling
348.79 SF Walls & Ceiling	106.84 SF Floor
11.87 SY Flooring	30.12 LF Floor Perimeter
41.37 LF Ceil. Perimeter	

Window	3' 6" X 4'	Opens into Exterior
Door	2' 6" X 6' 8"	Opens into LIVING_ROOM
Door	8' 9" X 6' 8"	Opens into FRONT_ROOM_C

DESCRIPTION	QUANTITY	UNIT PRICE	TAX	O&P	RCV	DEPREC.	ACV
1. R&R 1/2" drywall - hung, taped, floated, ready for paint	241.95 SF	2.63	9.73	129.22	775.28	(0.00)	775.28
2. Remove Vinyl floor covering (sheet goods)	106.84 SF	0.98	0.00	20.94	125.64	(0.00)	125.64
3. Vinyl floor covering (sheet goods) 15% waste added for Vinyl floor covering (sheet goods)	122.87 SF	3.65	20.58	93.82	562.88	(0.00)	562.88
4. R&R Carpet pad	106.84 SF	0.72	4.03	16.18	97.14	(0.00)	97.14
5. Remove Carpet	106.84 SF	0.29	0.00	6.20	37.18	(0.00)	37.18
6. Carpet 15% waste added for Carpet.	122.87 SF	3.58	26.65	93.32	559.84	(0.00)	559.84
7. R&R Interior door unit	1.00 EA	195.87	8.72	40.92	245.51	(0.00)	245.51
8. Paint door slab only - 2 coats (per side)	34.00 EA	33.10	18.11	228.70	1,372.21	(0.00)	1,372.21
9. Paint door or window opening - 2 coats (per side)	1.00 EA	27.86	0.32	5.64	33.82	(0.00)	33.82
10. R&R Baseboard - 2 1/4"	30.12 LF	3.52	1.92	21.60	129.54	(0.00)	129.54
11. R&R Outlet	5.00 EA	21.27	0.59	21.40	128.34	(0.00)	128.34
12. Paint casing - one coat	0.00 LF	0.85	0.00	0.00	0.00	(0.00)	0.00
13. R&R Outlet or switch cover	5.00 EA	3.66	0.23	3.72	22.25	(0.00)	22.25
14. R&R T & G paneling - knotty pine paneling (unfinished)	106.84 SF	5.95	15.30	130.20	781.20	(0.00)	781.20
15. Stain & finish paneling	106.84 SF	1.49	2.95	32.44	194.58	(0.00)	194.58
16. Seal/prime then paint the walls (2 coats)	241.95 SF	0.84	3.04	41.24	247.52	(0.00)	247.52
17. Paint the walls - one coat	241.95 SF	0.58	2.23	28.50	171.06	(0.00)	171.06
18. Paint baseboard - two coats	30.12 LF	1.30	0.28	7.90	47.34	(0.00)	47.34
19. R&R Wrap wood window frame & trim with aluminum sheet	1.00 EA	232.16	3.00	47.04	282.20	(0.00)	282.20
20. Seal & paint wood window (per side)	2.00 EA	50.00	0.86	20.18	121.04	(0.00)	121.04
21. R&R Window sill	3.50 LF	4.12	0.23	2.92	17.57	(0.00)	17.57
22. Seal & paint window sill	3.50 LF	2.31	0.06	1.64	9.79	(0.00)	9.79
23. R&R Ceiling fan & light	1.00 EA	363.42	10.68	74.82	448.92	(0.00)	448.92
24. R&R Rigid conduit, 1"	8.00 LF	15.09	1.88	24.52	147.12	(0.00)	147.12

Most public adjusters also use the Xactimate program to complete their estimates on behalf of the insured. This allows the public adjuster to easily do an estimate comparison between the two estimates. The estimate comparison happens when there is a major difference between the estimate completed by the public adjuster and the estimate completed by the insurance adjuster. For example, if the estimate completed by the public adjuster is $75,000 more than the estimate completed by the insurance adjuster, completing a comparison of the estimate is less complicated if the estimates are both completed on the same software. Before the public adjuster inputs the Xactimate program to do the estimate, he/she usually meets at the loss site with the insurance adjuster to try to reach an agreed scope. If the public adjuster and the insurance adjuster agree on the same scope, then the expectation is that their estimates will end up being relatively close to the same dollar amount. However, if they are both using the Xactimate program and they cannot agree on the scope, then it is up to the public adjuster to use his negotiating skills, knowledge and professional resources to get the insurance adjuster to acquiesce. This is where having an experienced public adjuster can make all the difference in the outcome of the dwelling settlement.

Matching Replacement Items – "Reasonably Uniform Appearance"

Deciding if a component of a dwelling can be repaired or replaced can be subjective. Another subjective component of a dwelling adjustment is determining if materials can be matched for visual uniformity. For instance, if a fire occurs in the garage of a home and smoke stains the walls throughout the interior of the home, the insurance adjuster is going to determine which interior walls need to be painted and which rooms only need to be cleaned. If the paint is three years old or older and the adjuster is going to paint walls in certain rooms, the question becomes, "will the walls that are painted with new paint match the color of the rooms that are cleaned with paint that is three years old?" Another example is when the insurance adjuster is replacing a twenty year old window in a room that is visible from the front elevation. The concern may be that the new window(s) matches the rest of the windows in the home. This issue can also apply to carpet, cabinets, wall textures, tile, linoleum, roof shingles, doors, and stucco in addition to other interior and exterior finishes. Section 2695.9. (a) 2 of the California Fair Claims Practices reads as follows:

When a loss requires replacement of items and the replaced items do not match in quality, color or size, the insurer shall replace all items in the damaged area so as to conform to a *reasonably uniform appearance.*

The matching issue frequently comes up between the public adjuster and the insurance adjuster when they are trying to reach an agreed scope. The DOI regulation is subjective when it refers to "reasonably uniform appearance." Happily, this issue normally gets resolved through negotiations. There is a common rule of thumb referred to as the "line of sight rule," which means that standing at the origin of a loss, if the materials inside the home are going to be replaced, they must visually match as far as the eye can see from the origin. Thus, if a fire starts in the living room and the carpet needs to be replaced, and standing from the origin in the living room you can see that carpet runs continuous into the family room and up the stairs, then that is where the carpet should be replaced. The line of sight rule would not be favorable for an insured if the carpet also ran into the upstairs hallway and all the bedrooms where it was not visually seen while standing in the living room. Despite the line of sight rule, a good public adjuster has a decent chance of getting all the carpet replaced through the art of persuasion, compromise or negotiations.

What is The Actual Cash Value vs. Fair Market Value?

As mentioned in Chapter 3, there is a high probability that your policy will allow the insurer to apply depreciation in the dwelling estimate. For example, within an Xactimate estimate, the scope may indicate that the carpet in the living room is being removed and replaced. Unless the carpet was brand new at the time of the loss, the insurance adjuster will apply and subtract an amount of depreciation for the material based on the age of the carpet at the time of the loss. Depreciation is applied to most materials that wear out over time. The depreciation is applied accordingly to the materials in the repair estimate. The outcome is that the estimate shows the cost or repairs at Replacement Cost with a deduction for the amount of the Depreciation to derive at the Actual Cash Value settlement.

When a home is a total loss, it is deemed unrepairable. Therefore, the courts in the State of California (Jefferson) have determined that the Actual Cash Value of a dwelling loss is not based on a repair estimate less applied depreciation for materials as explained above. Rather, the courts (Jefferson) have ruled that determining the Actual Cash Value is based on the Fair Market Value, meaning that the value is determined based on Market Value of the home as established by a Real Estate Appraisal. The insurance company will hire a Real Estate Appraiser to complete a valuation appraisal of the property based on comparable homes in the proximate market that have sold recently to the date of the appraisal. The value of the land will be subtracted from the appraisal to determine the Market Value of the dwelling at the time of the loss. The ACV settlement for the total loss structure will be the outcome of the Fair Market

What if My Home is a Total Loss?

The reason it is important to know this is because most people believe they will recover more money from their insurance company if their home is deemed a total loss. However, in most cases, especially in a depressed market, the Market Value of a home will be less than an Xactimate estimate of repairs with the deduction for depreciation of the materials. For example, a home damaged in a fire might have a Market Value of $100,000 compared to an Xactimate estimate to repair the home at a cost of $150,000 ACV. There are no laws or regulations used in the insurance industry for residential or commercial property claims to establish if a home is a total loss or repairable. The determination is subjective. Therefore, your insurance adjuster may try to convince you that your home is a total loss so he can apply the Fair Market Settlement which may be lower than a repair estimate minus deprecation. We have witnessed instances where the insurance adjuster deemed the structure a total loss and paid the ACV based on an appraised value of the home. We have been successful at reversing this, completing an Xactimate estimate for repairs, less depreciation, which resulted in a much higher ACV settlement. Thus, if you are experiencing this issue with your claims adjuster, try to find some portion of the structure that can be salvaged such as a wall or the foundation, and do not let the adjuster try to convince you that your home is a total loss.

What Is Dwelling Coverage – Detached Structures?

Under an insurance policy, Dwelling coverage may also cover other detached structures on the same property, such as sheds, pools, walkways, and fences. The limit for Other Structures is normally 10% of the limit for the main structure insured under the policy. Many of the same concepts covered in this chapter also apply to Other Structures. For example, if the paint and roof shingles on a detached garage match exactly with the exterior paint and roof shingles of the home, and the home is damaged by fire, but not the detached garage, the "line of sight" matching issue may come up for the paint and shingles on the detached garage that were not damaged by the fire. Note: Valued engineering and Fair Market Value also apply to Other Structures.

The General Contractor's Overhead & Profit

A dwelling estimate established on Xactimate should include an allowance for the general contractor's overhead and profit. The role of the general contractor is to select, coordinate, and monitor the work completed by the subcontractors. The general contractor usually commands a percentage fee based on the cost of the construction for the labor of the subcontractors and the material cost of the trade. The general rule of thumb is that the general contractor charges 10% for profit and 10% for overhead. For example, if the Xactimate estimate has $10,000 of the total cost of labor and material for the plumbing, then the estimate should also include an additional $1000 for profit and $1000 for overhead. There is, however, a provision in the standard Homeowners policy that excludes an insured from "profiting" from a covered claim. If the insured happens to be a general contractor or subcontractor and the insured wants to do the repairs, the insurance adjuster may try to deny the "profit" allocated in the Xactimate estimate. An insured who is a contractor would benefit by hiring a public adjuster to assure that he/she gets the 10% profit and to allow the contractor/insured to dictate the desired scope on the Xactimate program to tender the claim.

What You Should Know About Fire Restoration Solicitors

The fire and water loss repair and restoration business is a multibillion dollar industry. Repairing a home or building that has been damaged by a fire, water and smoke is a specialty type of construction that should be performed by a licensed General Contractor who specializes in repairing this type of damage. It takes a high level of experience to understand how to rid a home of smoke odor after a fire or to make sure that all the water is extracted. If you hire a contractor who does not have experience in fire, water and smoke restoration/construction, and he repairs the home, and it still smells like smoke or develops mold, insurance companies are not required to cover the cost to repair it a second time. It is much safer to hire a licensed General Contractor who is experienced with fire, water, and smoke mitigation and repairs if you have suffered a fire loss.

Unfortunately, anyone who suffers a fire loss is likely going to encounter a swarm of Fire Restoration Contractors soliciting to secure the job of repairing the home. There are usually multiple companies competing against each other to get the job to repair the damage or offer emergency services such as a "board up" or water mitigation. Occasionally emergency services are needed so it is not necessarily a bad thing for a contractor to solicit an insured immediately after a fire. However, some contractors are overly aggressive and intimidating in their approach. Unlike a public adjuster who has several rules and regulations regarding the solicitation of a loss, restoration contractors have few. For example, in the State of California under the Department of Insurance Regulations, it is illegal for a public adjuster to solicit a home or business owner until the fire department has left the scene of the fire. Also, a public adjuster can only solicit between the hours of 8am and 6pm. These are good rules.

However, restoration contractors do not have the same limitations which means it is open season for the contractors to hunt you down for a contract. If you hire a contractor to perform emergency services, it is important to make sure that your contract outlines the specific scope of the repairs. The contractor may try to convince you into believing that because you signed their contract for emergency services, you are committed to hiring their company to do all the needed repairs. Therefore, unless there is a need for emergency services, it is not necessary to hire a contractor immediately after a fire. Repairing your home and deciding who to hire is a big deal. Therefore, before you hire a contractor to do any repairs, you may want to get referrals and speak with others who have used their service. Also, it is worthwhile to check out their website and look them up with the state licensing board. In California, it is the CSLB at www.cslb.ca.gov.

Beware of Any Contractor Who Tells You He Can Handle Your Insurance Claim

Section 15007 of the California Insurance Commission defines a "public insurance adjuster" as "a person who, for compensation, acts on behalf of or aids in any manner, an insured in negotiating for or effecting the settlement of a claim or claims for loss or damage under any policy of insurance covering real or personal property or any person who advertises, solicits business, or holds him or herself out to the public as an adjuster of those claims."

Section 15006(a) of the California Insurance Commission states that no person shall engage in a business regulated under the Public Insurance Adjusters Act or act or assume to act as a public insurance adjuster unless he or she is licensed as a public insurance adjuster.

Therefore, in the State of California, it is against the law for any contractor (who is not a licensed public adjuster) to solicit or act as a public insurance adjuster as defined by the California Department of Insurance. If you experience anyone (including contractors) who solicit or act as a public adjuster, you can file a complaint on the California Department of Insurance website http://www.insurance.ca.gov.

Lastly, retaining a contractor immediately after a large property loss is not necessary without knowing what the construction budget is pending the outcome or settlement of the insurance claim. Unless you need immediate emergency services, you likely need the services of a public adjuster more than a General Contractor to complete the repairs.

CHAPTER 6

Contents Coverage and Deductible Pit Falls You Need To Know About

THE CONTENTS COVERAGE AFFORDED UNDER the Homeowners or Commercial property policy is intended to cover your personal belongings such as furniture, electronics, household items, tools, clothing, and things of that nature. Sometimes the lines get blurred between what is considered personal property and what is dwelling under the policy. For example, what about curtains? The rule of thumb is that if you were to sell your home, anything that would be included in the real estate sale would be considered dwelling and everything else inside the home is considered personal property. So then, since curtains usually are sold with the home, they are considered as dwelling and not as contents in the adjustment of a property claim.

The policy limit for your contents under a standard Homeowners policy is typically 75% of the limit for the dwelling. With most commercial property policies, the limit for contents is customized to reflect the total value of the business personal property (BPP).

A standard Homeowners policy contains several sub-limits for certain types of contents. For example, only $2500 for property used for business purposes: Supposing the insured was a plumber and there was $20,000 worth of tools that were damaged from a fire inside his garage. If the average insured, who does not know about the $2500 limit for business property, is asked by the adjuster what he does for a living and the insured answers that "he is a plumber," then the insurance adjuster may try to limit the settlement for the tools inside the garage to $2500. Suppose the insured retired twenty years prior to the fire? Can an argument be used that the tools do not qualify as property used for business and limited to only $2500? This is an example of how an insured can compromise a claim settlement based on something that was said without understanding how their answer could affect the outcome of the claim. There are several other limitations and conditions for contents under the standard Homeowner policy that an insurance adjuster can deploy to minimize the contents settlement.

The standard Homeowner and Commercial property policy contains the following policy language with regard to contents:

We will pay the cost to *repair* or *replace* covered contents, however, we will not pay an amount exceeding the smallest of the following;

1. The cost to replace at the time of the loss;

2. The full cost or repairs;

Here we go again! If you rely on your insurance company to make the determination whether a contents item can be repaired or requires replacement and/or determine the value of the settlement, you may be in for trouble.

Your insurance company will make the determination as to whether or not a damaged personal property item can be restored or if should be considered a total loss and replaced. It generally costs less to restore an item than cost to replace it. This provides the insurance company with an opportunity to minimize the contents settlement by insisting that a content item can be cleaned. There are many companies that are in the business of restoring contents after a fire or water loss. Many of these companies get their referrals from insurance adjusters. Over time, the adjuster and vendor may develop a mutually beneficial relationship that has the potential to become inappropriate, unprofessional, biased, and unethical. Without going into detail, some restoration companies are known to offer insurance adjusters free tickets for sporting events or concerts. Some restoration companies go as far as to offer all expense paid vacations to adjusters. Unfortunately, the temptation sometimes gets the best of the insurance adjuster, who may accept these unethical gifts. The insurance adjuster who falls into this is motivated to repay the restoration company with referrals. If the insured is claiming that a personal property item should be deemed a total loss, the insurance adjuster may lean on his restoration company of choice for an "opinion" that it can be cleaned to minimize the settlement. As a result, an insured may be forced to accept the cost of cleaning an item instead of the cost to replace it. As an example, an insurance adjuster may try to convince an insured that the electronics inside the home can be cleaned after a fire. The adjuster may pay the restoration company to pack them out, clean them, and return them. However, the problem with this is that many people do not recognize the long-term damaging effects that smoke exposure can have on sensitive electronic circuitry. It is possible that the smoke residue and odor can be eliminated from an electronic item after a fire. However, smoke exposure is highly corrosive to sensitive electronic circuitry which could cause the electronic item to fail after time and/or reduce its life expectancy. Below is the link to an article on this subject that will give a clear understanding of the damaging effects of smoke on electronics.

http://www.smithersrapra.com/SmithersRapra/media/Sample-Chapters/Practical-Guide-to-Smoke-and-Combustion.pdf

Beware of Asbestos

After a fire or other catastrophic even which causes damage to contents, an insured or a vendor may be in a hurry to remove them from the dwelling to mitigate the damage or begin restoration. This is highly discouraged as many homes constructed before 1978 were built with products that contain asbestos. Construction materials that often contain asbestos include drywall, linoleum, tile, roof shingles, and blown in insulation. If a home tests positive for asbestos and the asbestos is breached, then it is highly advisable not to remove items from the home or business unless you have consulted with a licensed asbestos abatement contractor first. For instance, if your home tested positive for asbestos located in the drywall and it was broken open (breached) by the heat from the fire or if the Fire Department knocked holes in the interior walls to extinguish the fire, then the asbestos particles may have been released into the air and likely spread throughout the entire interior of the home causing the asbestos particles to get into all soft goods such as clothing, cloth furniture, or anything that is considered porous. The asbestos particles can also get into small openings inside electronics. Additionally, due to the nature and the physical shape of the asbestos particulate, it cannot be removed from soft goods. Also, it is extremely difficult to remove asbestos from electronics. Therefore, all soft goods and electronics should be considered non-salvageable and a total loss. It is wise to be suspicious of restoration companies who are eager to pack out all your belongings before testing is completed. Nothing should be packed out until the home has been tested for asbestos.

Contents Valuation at Actual Cash Value and Replacement Cost

For contents claims, the standard Homeowners policy usually pays the Actual Cash Value (ACV) up front and then pays the Replacement Cost (R/C) when the item has been replaced. This concept is identical to the example that was used earlier for Dwelling losses. Allowing your insurance company to make the replacement cost or ACV determination is not going to be in your best interest and it is a conflict of interest.

After a fire loss, all the insured's total loss personal belongings need to be physically inventoried. Anything damaged beyond recognition needs to be added to the inventory. Once the inventory is completed, the Replacement Cost needs to be determined. Each item then needs to be depreciated based on the age and the condition. The result is an inventory that shows the Replacement Cost and the ACV amount of the settlement.

The *Replacement Cost* of a personal property item can range drastically in price depending on where it was purchased. For example, if the insured is claiming an alarm clock he purchased from a local retailor for $45, however, the same clock is selling for $20 on the internet. In this situation, the insurance companies use replacement cost resources that intentionally reduce the amount of the Replacement Cost. Some insurance companies get their pricing for free from internet companies in the hope that the internet company might get the sale when the insured replaces the item. If your insurance company determines that the Replacement Cost of the alarm clock is only $20 based on the web price, should you be forced to purchase it from an internet seller?

The determination of the Actual Cash Value is also subjective. In the State of California, the Department of Insurance Fair Claims Practices requires that the insurer must consider not only the age of the contents item, but also its *condition* in the determination of the amount of depreciation. Provision 2695.9 (3) f. of the California Department of Insurance Guidelines for Fair Claim Practices specifically states the following:

"(f) When the amount claimed is adjusted because of betterment, depreciation, or salvage, all justification for the adjustment shall be contained in the claim file. Any adjustments shall be discernible, measurable, itemized, and specified as to dollar amount, and shall accurately reflect the value of the betterment, depreciation, or salvage. Any adjustment for betterment or depreciation shall reflect a measurable difference in market value attributable to the <u>condition and age</u> of the property and apply only to property normally subject to repair and replacement during the useful life of the property. The basis for any adjustment shall be fully explained to the claimant in writing. «

Insurance companies use software programs that determine the amount of depreciation using a formula that takes into consideration the age and the condition of each item. Allowing your insurance company to determine the condition of your property may result in the ACV settlement being unfavorable to you. Not only should the insured be entitled to have a say in the condition of the property, he/she should also not be forced into accepting an ACV settlement based on software that is owned and operated by the insurance company. Most public adjusters use software that is programmed with a formula that minimizes the amount of depreciation based on the age and condition of an item. Relying on your insurance company to determine the amount ACV settlement of your contents claim is not recommended.

Beware of The Bankruptcy Land Mine

If an insured has ever filed for bankruptcy prior to a personal property claim, it could have a dramatic and catastrophic impact on the Contents claim. Anyone who files for bankruptcy must declare, under penalty of perjury, the approximate value of their personal property in the Bankruptcy filing. It is very common for the insurance company to perform a background check on an insured after they have filed a large property claim. If the insurance company becomes aware of a bankruptcy, the dollar amount that an insured declared in the bankruptcy filing for the value of the personal belongings will be used in the claim investigation. Because the value of the personal property assets was declared in bankruptcy court, the amount stated cannot be changed by the insured. Therefore, if the insured understated the value of their personal property at the time of the bankruptcy, the amount stated will be used in the claim investigation regardless of any excuses or explanations that the insured can come up with as to why the value should NOT be considered. This is called *judicial estoppel*. Since the insured declared the value of the personal assets during the bankruptcy proceedings, the insured is judicially estopped from changing the value with regards to the insurance claim.

To illustrate, let's use an example of an insured who filed a bankruptcy on December 31, 2015 and then had a fire loss on March 31, 2017. If the insured is claiming $150,000 at ACV and in 2015 declared in the bankruptcy that the value of the personal property assets was only $5000, the insured will be required to document/explain how they were able to acquire $145,000 worth of personal belongings/Contents between the filing of the bankruptcy and the date of the fire (2 years and 3 months). If the insurance adjuster took a recorded statement from the insured and asked what the yearly household income was and the insured answered $30,000 per year, then the question will become, how could the insured have acquired $145,000 in personal property in only 2 years and 3 months with an annual family income of $30,000.00 per year? The math will show that if the insured spent all the household income on personal belongings, they would only have $67,500.00 of total income to acquire $145,000 of personal belongings. In this situation, the claim would likely be assigned to the Special Investigative Unit for potential fraud. If the insurance company makes the determination that the amount of contents claimed by the insured is reasonably inconsistent with the amounts declared under penalty of perjury in the bankruptcy filing then the insurer can deny not only the contents on the basis of fraud, but the entire claim including the dwelling loss and the additional living expenses could also be denied.

With large loss claims involving contents, it is becoming standard operating procedure for the insurer to do a background check on the insured. If a bankruptcy was filed, the insurer will certainly try to use the judicial estoppel law to deny the claim or convince the insured that they should accept a reduced settlement to avoid a potential denial of the claim. public adjusters are your best advocate to help you navigate through any potential land mines one may encounter if there is a bankruptcy in the insured history.

CHAPTER 7

Additional Living Expense Claims

THE STANDARD HOMEOWNERS PROPERTY POLICY for an owner-occupied dwelling includes coverage for Additional Living Expenses (ALE). The limit is either a dollar amount or Actual Loss Sustained for a maximum number of months. For example, the limit may be $43,000 or a maximum of 12 months. When the limit is Actual loss sustained there is no dollar cap or limit. The coverage compensates the insured for the *additional* cost *incurred* to maintain the normal standard of living due to a covered cause of loss. The most common example of this is the insured whose home catches on fire and because of the damage, the home is not livable. Therefore, the insured must incur the expense of a rental home and continue to pay the mortgage while their home is being repaired. Thus, 100% of the expense to rent the home, including furniture, is compensable since the entire cost of the rental home is additional and incurred. Also, it is likely that before the insured moves into a rental home, time will be spent in a hotel. The cost to stay at the hotel is also completely covered under the ALE coverage.

Let's assume that the hotel does not have a kitchen or facilities to cook meals, and the insured will likely have to eat at restaurants. Only the *additional* cost to eat at the restaurant is covered under the ALE coverage. For example, if you had to eat at a restaurant and the bill was $20 and the same meal would have cost $7 to make at home, then the policy only covers the additional $13 which you incurred to eat the meal at the restaurant.

To make a claim for ALE, the insured is required to provide receipts as documentation that the expense was truly incurred. *ALE is one of the few coverages under the policy that require the insured to incur the expense before the claim is paid.* Collecting receipts and making copies of them is time consuming and cumbersome and probably the last thing an insured wants to remember to do after suffering a large fire loss. Some policies offer a substitute coverage called Fair Rental Value (FRV). FRV is the average rental value of the home. If the FRV of your home is $2000/month, the FRV coverage will pay you $2000/month for the *reasonable* amount of time that it takes to repair damage to your home from the covered cause of loss. If you decide to claim the FRV, you will automatically get the $2000/month and you do not have to document it with receipts or actually incur the expense. It is basically a cash-out form of coverage that is an option to the ALE. The disadvantage, however, is that if your actual ALE exceeds $2000/month, you won't be able to claim it since you elected the FRV instead.

Sometimes the ALE coverage presents an opportunity for the insured. For example, let's say that the policy has ALE coverage without the FRV option. So, if the insured wants to stay in a trailer that costs $30,000 the insured may be able to use some of the money available under the ALE coverage to purchase and keep the trailer. If a rental home and furniture was estimated to cost the insurer $3000 for eight months for a total of $24,000, the insured may be able to make a deal with the insurer, but only if it will save the insurer money on the ALE. The insurer may be willing to cash out $2000 a month for eight months for a total of $16,000 for the insured to use to fund the trailer and live in it, and then keep it at the end of the eight months. This arrangement allows the insured to fund $16,000 of the $30,000 cost of the trailer with the ALE proceeds, and it saves the insurer $8000. However, few people know this option might be available, and the policy does not address this.

Recovering Loss of Rent

When a Homeowner rents a home, the policy typically has coverage for the *Loss of Rents*. Since this part of the policy falls under the same category as the ALE, it is an incurred based coverage and the insured is required to document the loss of rental income loss as the Landlord. This means the insured will likely be requested to submit a copy of the lease agreement and copies of cancelled checks from the tenant in order to be compensated by the insurance company. As stated in Chapter 3, an insured is not allowed to profit from a covered loss under an insurance policy. If an insured was renting out a home for $1500/month and he paid the garbage that was $50/month, the net income would be $1450. If the Insurance adjuster asks the insured for any expenses that are discontinued due to the claim, the insured has the obligation to report the saved expenses. The insurance company has the right to subtract them from the monthly rent amount to make the claim payment. In the example above, the insurer would owe the insured $1450/ month.

Beware, There is a Time Limit

Coverage for the ALE, FRV and Loss of Rents is only for a *reasonable* time in which it takes to repair or replace the covered property. The word *reasonable* is subjective. To minimize the ALE/FRV or Loss of Rents loss, insurance adjusters may go out of their way to patrol and monitor construction. If the insurance adjuster forms the *opinion* that the repairs are taking longer than reasonable, the adjuster may threaten to terminate payments before the property is repaired. This situation can be very stressful for the insured. Suppose the adjuster does an estimate for the dwelling repairs and issues a payment for $50,000. The adjuster will likely believe the insured should start the repairs upon issuance of the payment. If the insured obtains an estimate from a general contractor to do the same scope of repairs as the adjuster's estimate and the contractor bid is $85,000, it would not be advisable for the insured to have the contractor start repairs. There should be a written contract between the insured and the contractor that specifies the scope and the total cost of the project. If the contractor bids $85,000 and the adjuster,s estimate is at $50,000, the insured would be foolish to secure a contract given the $35,000 shortage. The insured and the contractor may attempt to try to get the adjuster to increase his estimate, but this could take weeks or months. All the while the insured is not starting the project. The adjuster may be unwilling to increase his estimate and to make matters worse, the adjuster may threaten to stop paying the ALE as leverage to get the insured and the contractor to accept the $50,000. Sadly, this scenario plays out in real life all too often.

An important issue that comes up with regard to the ALE, is housing. ALE coverage is for the insured to maintain their desired standard of living. The determination of one's "standard" of living is subjective. If an insured has a home on the beach, should the insured be forced to accept a rental house without an ocean view? The insurance companies are looking for ways to cut claim spending, and the ALE housing provides the perfect opportunity to do just that. This situation gets stressful when the insured is staying in a hotel immediately following the loss while the search for a "suitable" rental home is in progress. Most people cannot wait to get out of the hotel and get into a rental home. It is very stressful for the insured when they find a suitable home available for rent and the insurance adjuster will not agree to pay the full amount of rent because the adjuster is of the "opinion" that the rental home is a betterment or an improvement of what is considered the insureds "normal standard of living."

Hopefully after reading this chapter, you understand how your insurance company can try to box an insured into accepting a low settlement or an inferior rental home in an effort to trim the ALE/FRV or Loss of Rents settlement.

Trying to handle this on your own may cause unnecessary stress as compared to getting the help you need from a public adjuster.

The Cash Advance

Sometimes an insured does not have the financial means to pay for a hotel while a rental home is being searched for if needed. Additionally, the insured may have lost all of their personal belonging in a fire and they may have nothing but the clothes they were wearing after the fire. If this is the case, the insured can request an advance form the insurance company. The advance should be requested out of the coverage for the contents because if the advance comes from the coverage for the dwelling, and there is a mortgage company listed on the policy, the check would include the mortgage company as a payee preventing the insured from being able to cash or deposit the check. Generally speaking, most insurance companies will advance an insured up to $5,000 from the Contents coverage so that the insured can purchase immediate needs such as clothing, cell phones, laptop computers, and toiletries. The advance will be subtracted from the amount of the Actual Cash Value contents settlement so don't think it is free money. Save your receipts so that when the contents inventory is completed, you can use the receipts for the purchases from the advance to claim replacement cost for those items since they have been replaced. Also, the insured can request that the insurance adjuster have the relocation housing set up direct pay at the hotel they are staying. This can usually be accomplished once someone from the insurance company (for example the adjuster) has physically inspected the loss and can verify that it is large enough to issue the advance and set up direct pay with the housing because the home is not livable.

As a reminder, the ALE coverage is an expense based coverage so the insurance company will likely not issue an advance against the ALE coverage. This is obviously a catch 22 considering the insured needs the funds, but they cannot get them because the expense (hotel fee, clothing, cell phone, etc.) has not been incurred.

There is nothing in the policy that requires the insurance company to issue an advance so remember it is gratuitous in nature. If there are any coverage issues or SIU "red flags" involved in the claim, the insurance company likely will not issue an advance. There are certain ways around this that a public adjuster may be able to navigate despite the coverage issues.

CHAPTER 8

Understanding Commercial Property Claims

THERE ARE MANY SIMILARITIES BETWEEN a residential property claim and a commercial property claim. Most of the principles, concepts and policy topics covered in this book apply to commercial property claims. There are, however, three main differences that distinguish a commercial property claim from a residential claim; policy forms; business income loss; and extra expense coverage.

What To Understand About Business Owners Policy (BOP)

Because there are a variety of types of businesses it makes it difficult to cover all or most with one basic standard coverage form. The smaller, less sophisticated businesses can be adequately covered under a common policy referred to as a Business Owners Policy (BOP). Another common policy for small and medium sized businesses is called a Commercial Property (CP). These two forms are common for small and middle sized businesses such as retail stores, restaurants, hotels, and some service type businesses. The BOP policy is tailored for smaller size businesses and the CP policy is more appropriate for middle sized companies. Moreover, each series of forms contains endorsements that can customize the coverage to cover the risk of the business. For instance, the BOP policy contains limited coverage for a customer's property when it is damaged while in the care or custody of the insured. There is a specific endorsement that provides broader coverage for property owned by customers. A laundromat, for instance, should purchase this endorsement to cover customers clothing in the event of a loss from a fire. There are dozens of endorsements available under the BOP or CP policies that allow the business owner to customize the policy coverage.

Larger and more complex businesses require broader and more sophisticated policies to cover the risk. For example, a factory with multiple locations and complicated machinery, supplies, products, and transportation equipment would not be adequately covered under a BP or a CP policy. The larger more sophisticated types of business are usually covered under a *manuscript policy*. The manuscript policy contains a general coverage form similar to the coverage form found in the BOP and CP forms. However, a manuscript policy contains dozens of unique endorsements that, together with the coverage form, customizes the coverage to provide adequate property and business income coverage. Some endorsements are even customized to meet the unique features of the business. These policies are commonly found for factories, clean rooms, lumber mills, and high tech software companies, to name just a few. Lastly, there is another type of commercial policy called *Inland Marine* that is common for the transportation industry. We could write an entire book on the topic of commercial policies and coverage, but with limited space and because the subject would generally not make for good reading, we will keep this topic limited.

Safeguard Provisions for Commercial Claims

Another element of coverage that is unique to a commercial property claim is a requirement called the *Safeguard Provisions*. The safeguard provisions is a requirement made by the insurance company that the insured is obligated to comply with before there will be coverage. An example of a safeguard provision is a working fire suppression sprinkler system in a building or a working alarm system. Safeguard provisions are required by the insurance company in an attempt to reduce the frequency of losses and to mitigate them. Considering that some commercial policies have policy limits in the tens of millions of dollars, it makes sense that the insurance company would require certain safeguard provisions in order to accept the risk of procuring the policy. However, it is the responsibility of the insured to comply with the safeguard provisions and make sure that whatever the provision is, it is properly working at the time of a catastrophe, such as a fire. If your business has suffered a large property loss, it is important that you review your policy to see if it contains any safeguard provisions so that you can be prepared to handle this issue when it comes up with the adjuster.

The Hazards of Coinsurance

As was noted in Chapter 2, paying insurance claims is the largest expense for any insurance company. The amount of income an insurance company makes is in large part from the Insurance premiums collected in addition to the amount the premium dollars made in the investment pool. The amount the insurance companies charge for premiums is based on the amount of the policy limits. If the limits are high so is the premium. If the limits are low, so is the premium. Because of this relationship between limits and premium, it is important for the insurance companies to make sure that the policy limits are not understated since it would reduce the amount of premium income. Obviously, if an insured understates a policy limit and then there is loss that is more than the limit, the insurance company would benefit. However, most claims are less than policy limits and, as such, the insurance companies must have a mechanism in place to ensure that policy limits are adequate to cover the amount of the loss, and more importantly, to ensure that the insurance company is collecting the maximum premium for their profitability. To achieve this goal, some insurance companies have a Coinsurance requirement.

The Coinsurance requirements can apply to Structures and Business Personal Property as well as Business Income.

The Declaration page of the commercial policy is where the Coinsurance requirement would be found if it was applicable. The Coinsurance requirement is a formula that requires the insured to have a policy limit that is within a certain percentage of the replacement cost value of the covered property. For example, if the insured has coverage for the Building with a limit of $100,000 and there is an 80% CoInsurance requirement, the insured is required to have a policy limit at least $80,000 or there will be a Coinsurance penalty. The Coinsurance formula is as follows:

Amount of Loss X (Limit of Insurance/Limits of Insurance Required) – Deductible = Loss Recovery. Below are some examples:

Example: Direct Damage

An insured owns a 25,000 square foot building that is 10 years old. He asks the builder to give him an estimate of what it would cost in 2017 to build the same structure from the ground up. He is told $80/square foot for a total estimated replacement cost of $2 million. He decides to insure the building to 90 percent of its estimated replacement cost value.

Scenario 1. A few months into the policy year, the building suffers a substantial fire loss, and the insured files a claim for $800,000. What is the insurance recovery after a $5,000 deductible?

Figure 1: Direct Damage Scenario 1

The replacement value of the building as determined by independent appraisal	$ 2,100.00
Coinsurance requirement	90%
Minimum Coinsurance Limit	$1,890.00
Insured limit	$2,000.00
Limit satisfies coinsurance minimum limit ($2,000.000/$2,1000.000)	YES
Reported loss	$800,000
Less coinsurance penalty	$0
Less deductible	($5,000)
Net insurance recovery	$795,000

Scenario 2. The insured decided at each renewal since 2012 that his building can remain insured for $2 million. The loss settlement clause remains replacement cost. The insured does not seek any independent counsel on the building's estimated replacement cost in 2016. The building is damaged by fire in mid-2016, and repairs total $500,000. The replacement cost of the building is determined to be $2.4 million. What is the insurance recovery after a $5,000 deductible?

Figure 2: Direct Damage Scenario 2

The repalcement value of the building as determined by independent appriasal	$ 2,400.00
Coinsurance requirement	90%
The coinsurance limit (insured value to insured limit)	$2,100,000
Insured limit	$2,000.00
Limit satisfies coinsurance minimum limit	NO
Reported loss	$500,000
Limit satisfies coinsurance minimum limit	0.926
Gross loss subject to insurance recovery	$463,000
Less deductible	($5,000)

If you have suffered a large commercial property loss, we urge you to review your policy Declarations sheet to see if you have a Coinsurance requirement. If you do, please consider the formula to do an initial assessment to determine if you may have a Coinsurance penalty. Please understand that the "limits of insurance required" portion of the formula is essentially an appraised or estimate value of the cost to build the structure from the foundation up for a building loss, or the cost to replace all the Business Personal Property at Replacement Cost, or the projected loss of Business Income. All three of these values can be subjective so if you find yourself with a Coinsurance issue, the best way to battle it is to do whatever you can to get the "limits of insurance required" as low as possible. Having an experienced public adjuster on your claim can help you avoid or minimize a potential Coinsurance penalty. There is a website that you can use to plug in the values to see if you may have a Coinsurance issue: https://www.claimspages.com/tools/coinsurance/

When Your Tenant Makes Improvements

Many small and middle sized business owners lease their buildings. Frequently, the business owner will customize the building to meet the needs of the business. When a tenant customizes the structure, these additions are called *tenant improvements and betterments* (TIB). For example, a business owner who leases a building for a retail business selling liquor might install (at the tenant's expense) a walk-in cooler, shelves, counters, and fancy displays that are all attached to the building. Obviously, the business owner as the tenant would want a property policy to cover the TIB as well as the business personal property (BPP) such as the inventory, cash registers, and cleaning supplies. Since the building is owned by the Landlord, the owner of the liquor store would not have an "insurable interest" in the building and would not be interested in insuring it. The TIB, however, is owned by the liquor store owner and needs to be covered under the BOP or CP policy. The BOP and CP policies provide coverage for the TIB under the BPP section of the coverage as long as it was purchased and installed to the building at the expense of the insured. This allows the owner of the liquor store to have coverage for the TIB affixed to the structure without having to insure the building. The lease agreement between the insured and the landlord would define who owns the TIB during the term of the lease and who is responsible for insuring it. Depending on how the lease agreement reads, the TIB may not be considered as the landlord's property and, as such they would not be interested in insuring it just like the tenant would not be interested in insuring the building. Most lease agreements stipulate that the TIB becomes the property of the landlord at the termination of the lease agreement. Therefore, during the period of the lease, the TIB is not technically owned by the landlord and should be insured by the tenant. This can cause a situation where the TIB is covered under both policies between the tenant and the landlord depending on how the lease agreement reads and the time frame of the loss in connection with the dates of the lease agreement. This situation is common in commercial property claims and it can complicate the adjustment. If the liquor store catches on fire, the insurance adjuster for the owner of the liquor store may conclude, after reading the lease agreement, that the TIB is the property of the landlord at the time of the loss and may deny payment to replace it. It would be wise if the owner of the liquor store had an advocate that could possibly interpret the lease agreement differently or find another argument that the TIB should be paid under his policy. It is possible that the TIB could be compensable under both policies for the tenant and the landlord.

What About Business Income Loss.

Another unique feature of a commercial property loss is Business Income. The financial exposure of the business income loss could be even greater than the dollar loss of the structure or the BPP. The property loss is tangible, you can easily see it, distinguish it, and it is relatively easy to quantify the cost to repair or replace it. The business income loss, however, is for the loss of <u>future earnings</u> due to a complete or partial shutdown of the operations. Therefore, it can only be based upon the historical financial performance of the business. Normally, the review of historical accounting data is used to project the future loss of the business income loss. The selection of the historical accounting data, the interpretation of it and how it will be used to predict the future business income loss makes the business income claim very subjective. Due to the subjective nature of the business income loss, the settlement frequently comes down to negotiations when the claim involves a public adjuster.

The Business Income covers the Gross Revenue loss minus any non-continuing expenses during the period of restoration. In other words, the business income coverage pays for the profit loss during the time the business is inoperable during the time it takes to repair or replace the covered property. Let's illustrate this with the example of a liquor store that is destroyed from a fire that occurred on February 1, 2016 and it takes a total of eight months to complete repairs during which time the business was completely discontinued. The only way to project the eight months of gross revenue loss is to use historical accounting data for the same time period. The Profit and Loss Statement (P&L) is frequently used to review the historical performance of the business assuming the books are honest and accurate. Let's say the insured's P&L shows that the gross revenue for the same eight-month period the year before the loss totaled $100,000. If history repeats itself, we can say that the insured's revenue loss for the eight-month suspension will be $100,000 of gross revenue. Now we need to subtract the non-continuing expenses to determine the profit loss. Obviously, the cost of the liquor will not be incurred by the insured for the eight months that the store is closed. If the P&L shows the total cost of the liquor was 30% of the gross revenue, then $30,000 would be deducted and the insurance company would pay $70,000 to settle the claim. This example illustrates the gross revenue minus non-continuing expense model.

The limits for Business Income coverage is either a stated dollar amount or it is for Actual Loss Sustained (ALS) usually for 12 to 24 months regardless of the dollar amount. The BOP policy usually contains a business income limit for 12 months ALS. The CP and the Manuscript policies usually have a dollar limit. Regardless of the limit or which commercial policy contains the business income coverage, the business income claim evaluation is always the same as described in the last paragraph. That is to say, historical accounting data is used to project the future business income loss during the period of restoration. The example of the liquor store was simplified to get the basic point across. The reality is that most business income projection and calculations are much more complicated. Often, the historical accounting data reveals upward and downward fluctuations of the gross revenue on a monthly or yearly basis. The selection of the historical accounting data can impact the loss calculation. Additionally, some expenses may or may not continue, subject to the opinion of the insured, and the insurer. *The selection and determination of what historical accounting data to use and the determination of what expenses should be considered, continuing and non-continuing, makes the business income projection very complex.*

Forensic Accountants are the CSI for Business Income

Your insurance company will likely hire a Forensic Accountant to project the business income loss. A Forensic Accountant is one who relies on historical accounting data to "project" the business income loss into the future during the period of restoration. As mentioned earlier, sometimes the historical data will have fluctuations or cycles. The decision of the Forensic Accountant with regard to the historical data to be used and how far back to go can have an effect on the business income loss projections. For example, if the historical data fluctuates over a three-year period and it shows a downward projection of 5% in gross revenue compared to a review of the prior two years that shows an increase in gross revenue of 3%, which data should be used to calculate the business income loss? The accountant hired by the insurance company likely will recommend using the historical data going back three years. Obviously, this would not benefit the insured, who should argue that the last two years of historical accounting data is more representative of the financial performance and should be used instead of 3 years of data. The determination of which expenses should be considered continuing or non-continuing can also get complicated. For example, the insured may argue that the cost of his employee labor should be a continuing expense so he can pay his employees during the eight-month shut-down to retain them and avoid having to hire and train new employees when the business re-opens. Since this issue involving *employee labor* is so frequent, many policies cover employee labor under the business income coverage. What about depreciation? Should depreciation on furniture, fixtures, and equipment be considered as continuing or non-continuing expense in the business income calculation? The answer might surprise you.

Forensic Accountants may also try to use *Market Data* to decrease the projected business income loss. As an example, if the insured owns an ice cream parlor and has a business income claim for the complete suspension of his business, there could be market data regarding public consumption trends of Americans who eat ice cream. For example, when the World Trade Center was destroyed in 911, there was market research on ice cream consumption in America which showed that Americans consumed a higher percentage of ice cream for roughly 3 months after 911 because it was a comfort food. Four months after 911, the percentage of ice cream consumption drastically decreased when Americans started their diets to lose the weight. If your business income loss occured shortly after 911, the accountant hired by your insurance company may use the market data to minimize the business income loss projection. The Forensic Accountant hired by your insurance company will be on the lookout for accounting data fluctuations and market data trends that can be relied upon to minimize your business income claim. A public adjuster might be able to discredit such trends resulting in a higher business income settlement.

How Can I Get Extra Expenses?

The coverage for Extra Expense is contained within the same part of the commercial policy as the Business Income coverage. Extra Expense covers any expense that allows the insured to resume or partially resume operations, that are suspended due to a covered cause of loss, as long as the expense reduces the business income loss by an amount equal to or greater than the amount of the extra expense. If you understand this, then you can see that the extra expense coverage is mutually beneficial to the insured and the insurer. As an example, using the liquor store mentioned earlier, if the business income loss exposure to the insurer is $70,000 for an eight-month period, but after the first month following the loss, the insured wants to claim $40,000 under extra expense for the cost to temporarily relocate the store, the insured would save the insurer $21,250. Since the opportunity for the insured to temporarily relocate the liquor store was not realized until one month after the fire, the insured would have paid one month of business income which totals $8750. The cost of the first month of business income plus the $40,000 relocation expense means that the insurer would pay the insured a total of $48,750 compared to $70,000 (a savings of $21,250) for eight-months of business income if the store was not relocated. If the insured moves to a new location under the extra expense coverage and the sales are less than what they were projected to be at the original location for the total eight-month time period, then the insurer would pay the extra expense and business income loss at the new location, but would not pay more than $70,000 combined.

Convincing an insurer to pay extra expense means the insured must demonstrate that it will save the insurer on the business income loss. If the data is subjective, convincing the insurer to pay for the extra expense can be very complicated and even stressful. It's bad enough the insured suffered a property loss that caused the complete or partial shutdown of the business operations and now the insured is in a position where a plan of action is developed to "stop the bleeding." The insurer won't agree to pay for it because they are not convinced that the extra expense will save them money. Imagine your insurance company is projecting a small business income loss. You know better, but your insurance company is not willing to pay for extra expense because the extra expense "appears" to be more than the projected income loss. Therefore, it makes sense during a commercial loss to have an advocate in your corner such as a public adjuster.

Extended Period of Indemnity

Most commercial policies offer a business income coverage feature referred to as Extended Period of Indemnity (EPI). When a business is closed for several months for the repair or replacement of the covered property, the business income coverage is compensating the insured for the business income loss. When the business re-opens, there still might be a business income loss as the business ramps back up to its pre-loss level. It is very common for a business to take weeks or months after it re-opens to get all the customers back and to get the gross income to where it was prior to the loss. Therefore, the EPI compensates the insured for the time it takes the business to recover 100% of its gross revenue after the business opens. Most EPI coverages provide 30 to 90 days of coverage. That means that after the business opens, the Forensic Accountant hired by the insurance company will monitor the post opening accounting data and compare it to the projections based on the historical accounting data in order to calculate the EPI loss.

Like Commercial Policies, we could write an entire book on the subjective of the business income claims. Hopefully this chapter helps you to understand how the accounting data is selected and how the data interpreted in the calculation of the business income loss is subjective and can have a substantial effect on the loss projection. This situation is even exascerbated by the complexity of some of the business income policy forms. This creates the opportunity for the accountant hired by an insurance company to minimize the amount of your business income loss settlement. A good public adjuster will know how to combat this from happening.

CONCLUSION

WHILE THE PROBLEMS WITH CLAIMS handling are complicated and intentionally favor the insurance companies best interest, this book has been written to be a source of reference for you to gain quick answers to the many questions you may have while negotiating an insurance claim.

We believe there is no substitution for professional help during the claim process. As the saying goes, "you would not go into court without an attorney, so why would you take on your insurance company without representation?"

We wish you the best in this journey, and we are here to assist you (hold your hand) throughout the process.

If you have any questions or if you find that the information in this book has convinced you that a large loss claim is not for the untrained, I encourage you to contact us through our website or directly by calling us.

Independence Public Adjusters, Inc.
AZ Lic# 1039385 · CA Lic# 2109693
5183 Lone Tree Way
Antioch, CA 94531
www.independencepublicadjusters.com
steve@theipa.us
tony@theipa.us
925-826-7500
925-432-4989

ABOUT THE AUTHORS

Anthony (Tony) Astone

After graduating from San Jose State University in 1991, I took my first job in the insurance industry as a entry level property adjuster for one of the largest insurance companies. Over the next 17 years I worked my way up the position of

Executive General Adjuster where I handled multi-million dollar commercial and residential property claims throughout the United States. At one point I was a Property Claim Manager for 3 years overseeing 9 adjusters who specialized in Mold and Special Investigative property claims.

In 2008 I crossed the fence to become a public adjuster and in 2012 started Independence public adjusters, Inc., with my partner Steve Boydstun. My experience working for the insurance companies provides me with the insight and knowledge to be one step ahead of the insurance adjusters that I now face on a daily business. As they say, the best way to beat the opposition is to know the opposition. Combined with my 9 years as a public adjuster, I can competently and proficiently handle a wide range of small and large residential and commercial claims to the satisfaction of our Clients with the goal of maximizing each recovery and reducing the stress.

Steve Boydstun

I am a licensed public adjuster and co-founder of Independence Public Adjusters, Inc. ("IPA"), a public adjusting firm that helps clients receive more favorable recoveries for their home or commercial insurance claims. Before devoting myself full-time to IPA, I was a commercial pilot for Ameriflight, Community Air, and Horizon Airlines, where he enjoyed traveling the western states and Canada. After the birth of my second son and a desire to be home with my family, a change was made to become a manufacturer representative for large companies such as CertainTeed, Graphic Sciences, and Cummins-Allison. In 2011, I joined Tony Astone and we formed IPA, where we now work to ensure that our clients receive the best possible settlment of their insurance claims.

SPECIAL FREE BONUS GIFT FOR YOU

To help you achieve more success, there are FREE Bonus Resources for you at:

www.IPA.com/FreeGiftFrom

THE IDEAL PROFESSIONAL SPEAKER FOR YOUR NEXT EVENT

Any organization and their employees that want to learn more about how to prepare for the insurance game needs to hire Tony or Steve for a keynote and /or workshop training
To Contact or book Tony or Steve to Speak: 5183 Lone Tree Way, Antioch, CA 94531 | PHONE: 925.325.4989 or 925.826.7500 | FAX: 925.755.0556

WHEN THE SMOKE CLEARS

"Share This Book"

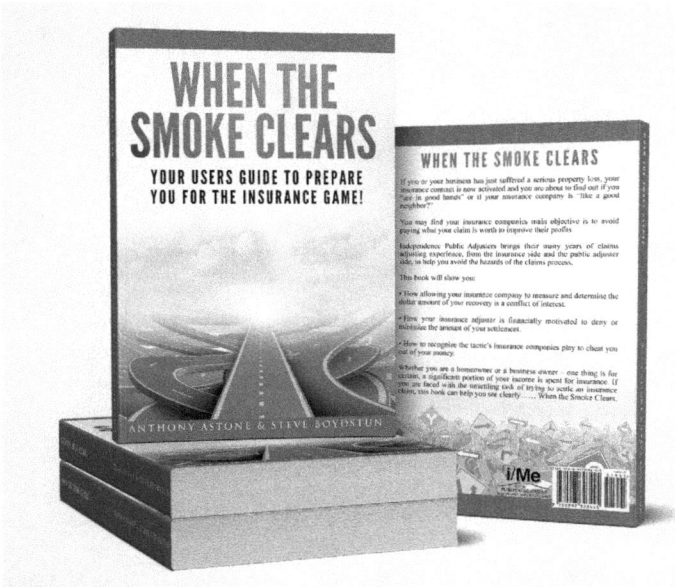

Retail 19.95

Special Quantity Discounts

5-20 Books	17.95
21-99 Books	16.95
100-499 Books	14.95
500-999 Books	10.95
1,000+ Books	8.95

To Order Go To www.Independencepublicadjusters.com

www.ingramcontent.com/pod-product-compliance
Lightning Source LLC
Chambersburg PA
CBHW060548100426
42742CB00013B/2495